The German Christmas Cookbook

The German Christmas Cookbook

Traditional bakes, biscuits and feasts
for festive celebrations

Jürgen Krauss

K

First published in Great Britain in 2025
by Kyle Books, an imprint of
Octopus Publishing Group Ltd
Carmelite House
50 Victoria Embankment
London EC4Y 0DZ
www.octopusbooks.co.uk

An Hachette UK Company
www.hachette.co.uk

The authorized representative in the EEA
is Hachette Ireland, 8 Castlecourt Centre,
Dublin 15, D15 XTP3, Ireland
email: info@hbgi.ie

Text copyright © Jürgen Krauss 2025
Design and Layout copyright
© Octopus Publishing Group Ltd 2025
Photography copyright
© Maja Smend 2025

All rights reserved. No part of this work
may be reproduced or utilized in any
form or by any means, electronic or
mechanical, including photocopying,
recording or by any information storage
and retrieval system, without the prior
written permission of the publisher.

Jürgen Krauss asserts the moral right to
be identified as the author of this work.

ISBN 978-1-80419-284-9

A CIP catalogue record for this book
is available from the British Library.

Printed and bound in China

10 9 8 7 6 5 4 3 2 1

Publisher Jo Copestick
Senior Editor Alex Stetter
Art Director Jaz Bahra
Photography Maja Smend
Food Styling Katie Marshall
Props Styling Tony Hutchinson
Production Manager Caroline Alberti

Illustrations Ekaterina Koniukhova/
Shutterstock

Contents

Introduction 6
Biscuits 10
Cakes and Tarts 72
Bread – Sweet and Savoury 98
Festive Meals 120
Christmas Market Food 168
From the German Pantry 190

Index 202
Thank you 207

Introduction

It gets very dark early now, at this time of the year. At the narrow spot of the Kappel Valley where my childhood home stands, the sun disappears behind the ridge just after lunch and sets around 5pm, unseen by us. The cold outside tries to creep in, and we children watch ice flowers grow on the panes of the kitchen window.

But our small kitchen is warm and cosy, heated by a woodburning stove. The air in the valley and in our house is full of the scents of log fires, and soon there will be others mingling in: the scent of cinnamon, cloves, cardamom and of freshly baked biscuits will fill the air – it is Advent, the time to prepare for Christmas.

During my childhood, this period of preparation and anticipation was a rather intimate time. There were the occasional visits to Freiburg with its small, cosy Christmas market and snow-crystal streetlights, but due to the early onset of darkness, there was more time indoors – family time spent playing card games and board games, watching TV together and, of course, preparing food and baking.

Come with me to visit my memories of food and other activities that made Advent so special.

In our household, as in most German families, the most wonderful thing about the weeks leading up to Christmas was always the abundance of Christmas biscuits. Prepared throughout the Advent period, which begins on the Sunday closest to 30 November, these special biscuits are designed to keep well, and their flavours improve over time. Biscuits therefore play a particularly prominent role in this book, from chocolate pretzels that make perfect gifts to a Black Forest-style gingerbread farmhouse, complete with a balcony.

The dishes traditionally served on Christmas Eve or Christmas Day in Germany vary from region to region. My parents, however, were always a bit experimental in the kitchen at this time of year, when they had more time than usual to prepare the food we were going to eat, and they didn't stick to tradition much. Our Christmas meals would instead be created from locally sourced ingredients, for example fish caught by my father, or some game that was offered to us by our family physician, an avid hunter. This is why the suggested holiday meals in this book are not strictly traditional German Christmas menus – rather, they reflect the customs of my own childhood home.

Intricately linked with my memories of the Christmas season are my memories of the other things that always made this time of year special, which range from getting ready for our town band's annual Christmas concert to the TV programmes we watched every year without fail. The family preparations for Christmas usually started at the beginning of December, but for me the Christmas season, with its cold weather, long nights and special food, always began around 11 November, with the lantern processions held for St Martin's Day, and ended on 6 January, with Epiphany, when the Christmas tree would be taken down.

I hope you enjoy my recipes and stories from this special time.

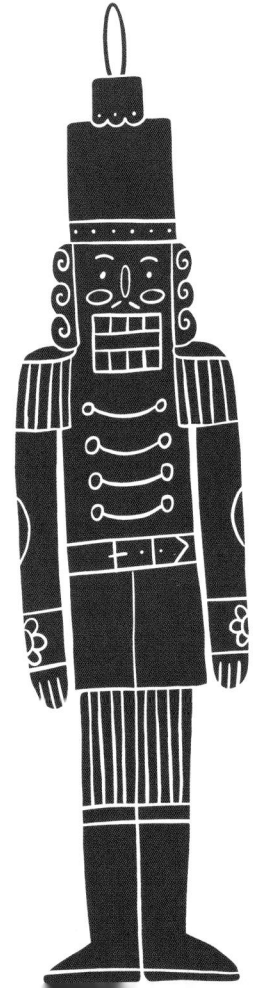

Biscuits

Haselnuß-Makronen
Hazelnut Macaroons 15

Kokos-Makronen
Coconut Macaroons 16

Butter-Gebäck
Butter Biscuits 19

Bethmännchen
Little Bethmanns 20

Gefüllte Hörnchen
Swaddled Biscuits 22

Zimtsterne
Cinnamon Stars 25

Nuss-Kaffee-Plätzchen
Walnut and Coffee Biscuits 26

Linzer Weihnachtsplätzchen
Linzer Christmas Biscuits 29

Schwarz-Weiß-Gebäck
Black and White Biscuits 30

Anis-Plätzchen
Aniseed Biscuits 33

Spritzgebäck
Piped Biscuits 34

Rum-Kugeln
Rum Balls 39

Vanille-Gipfele
Vanilla Crescents 40

Pistazien-Plätzchen
Pistachio and Orange Biscuits 43

Hilda-Brötle 44

Schoko-Brezeln
Chocolate Pretzels 47

Marzipankartoffeln
Marzipan Potatoes 48

Feine Lebkuchen
Special Gingerbread 51

Gefüllte Lebkuchen-Herzen
Filled Gingerbread Hearts 53

Honig-Lebkuchen
Honey Gingerbread 54

Käseplätzchen
Cheese Biscuits 57

Springerle 58

Lebkuchenhaus
Gingerbread House 63

The house I grew up in was typical of the kind you find in small Black Forest villages. Half the house was originally a barn, with space for some animals, but this traditional house had eventually been converted into four flats and was now occupied by three generations of the Ringwald family (my mother's side).

Everyone enjoyed making biscuits during the time before Christmas. Close as the families were, I only remember making biscuits with my mother and brother, but of course we eventually got to sample everybody else's. Each part of the family had their own way of doing things, and for that reason the process of making biscuits felt like something intimate, almost secretive – special time spent with the closest of relatives.

Many Germans follow this tradition during Advent. These biscuits keep well and are stored in tins until they are either served to visitors or given as Christmas gifts.

This is a delicious, gluten-free staple found on German coffee tables at Christmas. Although these are less sticky than the Coconut Macaroons on page 16, it's still a good idea to bake them on traditional German baking wafers, known as *Back Oblaten*, or on a sheet of rice paper. You can cut the rice paper into small squares in advance, but it's not strictly necessary as the paper will tear into roughly macaroon-shaped pieces when the baked biscuits are lifted off at the end. If you can't get hold of rice paper, nonstick baking paper works well too.

Haselnuß-Makronen
Hazelnut Macaroons

Preheat the oven to 150°C fan/gas mark 2. Line 2 baking sheets with 35 *Back Oblaten* (round German baking wafers, 4cm in diameter), or 2 large sheets of rice paper, cut into small squares, or nonstick baking paper.

Whisk the egg whites into soft peaks in a big bowl. Add the icing sugar bit by bit, whisking as you do so, and continuing to whisk until each addition has dissolved completely. Fold in the ground hazelnuts and cinnamon.

Using 2 teaspoons or a piping bag fitted with a 1.5cm plain nozzle, place or pipe small mounds of the mixture onto your prepared sheets, setting them about 3cm apart. Push a whole hazelnut into the centre of each mound.

Bake for about 25 minutes, until the macaroons are just a little bit soft and chewy in the centre. Set aside to cool on a wire rack, then store in an airtight container, where they will keep for several weeks.

MAKES ABOUT 35

2 egg whites
120g icing sugar
160g ground hazelnuts
¼ teaspoon ground cinnamon
about 35 whole hazelnuts,
   for decorating

These little mounds of tropical goodness were a favourite of my grandma Ida. On attending my first Passover service at my in-laws' house, I found they were also popular in Jewish communities over this festival period because they are made without flour. Being very sticky, they are best made on German baking wafers or rice paper (see page 15).

Kokos-Makronen
Coconut Macaroons

MAKES ABOUT 40

2 egg whites
75g caster sugar
120g desiccated coconut
1 teaspoon lemon juice
zest of 1 lemon
dark chocolate, as required

Preheat the oven to 140°C fan/gas mark 3. Line 2 baking sheets with 40 *Back Oblaten* (round German baking wafers, 4cm in diameter), or 2 large sheets of rice paper, cut into small squares, or nonstick baking paper.

Whisk the egg whites into soft peaks in a big bowl. Add the caster sugar bit by bit, whisking as you do so, and continuing to whisk until each addition has dissolved completely. Fold in the desiccated coconut, then fold in the lemon juice and zest.

Using 2 teaspoons or a piping bag fitted with a 1.5cm plain nozzle, place or pipe small mounds of the mixture onto your prepared sheets, setting them about 3cm apart. If desired, you can wet your fingers and shape the macaroons into little mountains.

Bake for 25–30 minutes, until the tips of the mountains become a light golden colour. Set aside to cool completely on a wire rack.

Place the chocolate in a heatproof bowl and microwave on High in 10-second bursts, stirring after each burst, until it has the desired consistency. Alternatively, you can use a bain-marie: sit the bowl over a pan of simmering water – it must not actually touch the water – and stir as it melts. With both methods, the chocolate should not get warmer than 34°C. Dip the macaroons into the bowl to coat them fully or partly, or drizzle the chocolate over them with a spoon.

These macaroons tend to absorb moisture from the air, so will keep in an airtight container for just about a week. However, they are likely to be eaten long before that.

As children, my brother and I particularly looked forward to making these biscuits, because there were no rules about how to shape and decorate them. I believe we made many Santas and Christmas trees over the years, and also some less recognisable shapes, sculpting the dough freehand with our small fingers! But we always made enough of the more usual types – biscuits glazed with egg yolk and sprinkled with sugar pearls, or drizzled with lemon icing or melted chocolate – to serve to visitors and give as presents.

Butter-Gebäck
Butter Biscuits

Preheat the oven to 180°C fan/gas mark 6. Line 2 baking sheets with baking paper.

Using an electric mixer, cream the butter and sugar together. Once combined, mix in the cream, liqueur, lemon zest and salt.

Mix in the flour until a smooth dough forms but take care not to overmix. You can use this dough immediately or cover with clingfilm and leave to rest in the fridge until needed, for up to three days.

To make the biscuits, roll out the dough on a floured surface until about 3mm thick. Using whatever size and shape of cutter you like, stamp out shapes and transfer them to the baking sheets.

For a simple glaze, brush with beaten egg yolk, then decorate as desired with sugar crystals or sprinkles that won't melt in the oven. If you want to decorate your biscuits with melted chocolate (see page 16) or the lemon glaze, do not brush them with egg yolk first. Bake for 8–10 minutes, then transfer to a wire rack and set aside to cool.

If you would like your biscuits to have a lemon glaze, bake them first, as above. Meanwhile, put the icing sugar into a bowl and stir in some lemon juice, adding small quantities at a time, until it is thick enough to brush onto the biscuits without running off. Apply the icing thinly, then decorate as you wish. Let the glaze dry before storing the biscuits.

If stored in an airtight container, these biscuits will keep well for several weeks.

MAKES 50–80,
DEPENDING ON CUTTER SIZE

125g cold unsalted butter, cubed
125g caster sugar
1 tablespoon double cream
2 teaspoons almond liqueur or rum
zest of 1 lemon
1 pinch salt
250g plain flour, plus extra for dusting
1 egg yolk, beaten, to glaze

To decorate
sugar crystals, coloured if you like
sprinkles (check they won't melt in the oven)
chocolate, as required

For the lemon glaze (optional)
100g icing sugar, sifted
lemon juice

These biscuits were probably invented in honour of the German Bethmann banking family in around 1830. They are surprisingly simple to make, taste delicious and keep for a long time. To make this recipe gluten-free and vegan, swap the plain flour and egg for cornflour and egg replacer.

Bethmännchen
Little Bethmanns

MAKES ABOUT 30

300g homemade Marzipan (see page 192), or 200g ready-made marzipan (with 25 per cent almonds) plus 100g ground almonds
75g icing sugar
60g plain flour
1 egg
1 teaspoon almond extract
100g blanched almonds, split in half
1 egg yolk, beaten

Break the marzipan into small pieces and place in a bowl. Add the extra ground almonds if using ready-made marzipan, then add the sugar, flour, whole egg and almond extract. Stir to combine, then knead until a smooth ball forms. Wrap the dough in clingfilm and leave to rest in the fridge for about 30 minutes.

Preheat the oven to 160°C fan/gas mark 4. Line a baking sheet with baking paper.

Divide the dough into walnut-sized pieces. Roll each piece into a ball and place it on the prepared sheet. Decorate each piece with 3 equally spaced almonds, pointed ends towards the middle. Brush with beaten egg yolk to glaze.

Bake for 15–20 minutes, until the tops are golden in colour. Set aside to cool, then store in an airtight container, where they will keep for about 3 weeks.

St Nicholas Day

In Germany, as in much of Western Europe, 6 December is dedicated to the memory of Bishop Nicholas of Myra, the patron saint of sailors, merchants and children, who died on this day nearly 1,800 years ago. (Sources are precise about the day, less so about the year.) Over the centuries, tales of his generosity led to St Nicholas being associated with gift-giving, and so the tradition developed that he comes to people's houses on 6 December, asks the children if they have been well-behaved and brings them some gifts.

After the Reformation, some Protestant scholars thought that St Nicholas was getting too much attention and the gift-giving was shifted from 6 December to Christmas, with the *Christkind*, or Christ Child, becoming the bringer of gifts. But many children still receive small gifts on St Nicholas Day in Germany, as well as in the Netherlands and Belgium, where the gift-giver is known as *Sinterklaas* – a name that may sound familiar to English speakers.

In many places, St Nicholas arrives dressed as a bishop, carrying a staff. He is usually accompanied by a scary helper or two – characters that probably date back to pre-Christian times. In our town, his helper was Knecht Ruprecht, a frightening-looking man who carried a sack full of gifts for the well-behaved children, but also birch canes with which to threaten those who had been naughty.

When I was a boy, the arrival of these characters was met with a mixture of excitement and nervousness. We children were looking forward to getting gifts – mostly sweets and oranges – but there was also the slightly uncomfortable prospect of what St Nicholas might find written in his big golden book, which was filled with all the details of things we'd done throughout the year. If we had been naughty, there was the threat of Knecht Ruprecht and his canes... although he never actually used them on any children. In fact, on closer examination, they had little bundles of chocolates tied to the ends. (The canes were available for sale at the shop next door!)

As I got older, I realized that St Nicholas and Knecht Ruprecht were just students who had been hired to dress up and play the part. My mother likes to tell the story about how she learned the truth about St Nicholas when she was little. One year on 6 December, there was a knock on the door and in came St Nicholas and Knecht Ruprecht. Her older sister, my aunt Olga, must have noticed something about their outfits. She went to a window from which she could see the shed behind the house and shouted, 'They're fake! Ruprecht is wearing the old coat and boots that have been in the shed for ages!'

My great-grandmother, 'Oma Berta', with St Nicholas consulting his book.

Here, pieces of nut paste are swaddled in biscuit dough – an easy variation on Butter Biscuits (see page 19) but with a very different look and taste. In this case they are also decorated with icing, which can be flavoured and coloured as you wish.

Gefüllte Hörnchen
Swaddled Biscuits

MAKES 30

100g homemade Marzipan (see page 192, or use ready-made), or Pistachio Paste (see page 192)
2 teaspoons almond liqueur
icing sugar, if needed
flour, for dusting
1 quantity rested Butter Biscuit dough (see page 19)
1 egg, beaten, for egg wash

For the icing
icing sugar
water, lemon juice or liqueur of your choice
food colourings (optional)

Knead the marzipan or nut paste to soften it, then knead in the almond liqueur. If the marzipan gets very soft, add a bit of icing sugar. The consistency should be pliable, not sticky.

Preheat the oven to 180°C fan/gas mark 6. Line 2 baking sheets with baking paper.

Divide the marzipan into 30 cherry-sized pieces and roll each one into a bean shape.

Lightly flour a work surface and roll out the butter biscuit dough until about 3mm thick. Cut into 30 squares of 4 x 4cm.

Place a marzipan bean diagonally at the centre of each square. Pull one corner of the square over the long side of the marzipan bean, then pull over the opposite corner and stick it down with egg wash. Do this with all the squares.

Place the biscuits on the prepared sheets, spacing them about 2cm apart, and bake for 8–10 minutes. Set aside to cool.

Once cool, make a slightly runny icing by mixing icing sugar with a small amount of water, lemon juice or liqueur of your choice. If you wish, portions of the icing can be placed in separate bowls and coloured with food colouring. Apply the icing to the corners last pulled over, this should result in an iced triangle.

The flavour of these biscuits improves over time, and they will keep in an airtight container for several weeks.

Very easy to make, and a staple in every German household around Christmas time, cinnamon stars are naturally gluten-free, and were among my grandma's favourites. It's impossible to overwork the dough, so these are a great bake if you have children involved, or are at the start of your baking journey. If possible, use almonds with the skin on and grind them yourself – the stars will have a richer flavour and better colour.

Zimtsterne
Cinnamon Stars

Preheat the oven to 150°C fan/gas mark 2. Line a baking sheet with baking paper.

Put the almonds into a bowl with the cinnamon, add the icing sugar and mix well. Stir in the egg white, then knead with your hands until you get a smooth ball.

Dust a work surface with a little extra icing sugar and roll out the dough until 1cm thick. Using a star-shaped cutter of your preferred size, stamp out stars and transfer them to the baking sheet.

Using an electric mixer, beat the egg white for the icing into stiff peaks. Add the icing sugar bit by bit while continuing to whisk. Finally add the rum.

Use this meringue mixture to paint the stars evenly. The thickness of the meringue is a matter of taste, but it should cover only the top of the stars, not the sides.

Bake for 10–15 minutes – the meringue should still be white – then set aside to cool. The stars are quite delicate at first, but develop a slightly chewy texture while cooling. If stored in an airtight container, they will improve over time and keep for at least 6 weeks.

MAKES ABOUT 40,
DEPENDING ON CUTTER SIZE

250g ground almonds (skin on)
1 teaspoon ground cinnamon
150g icing sugar, plus extra for dusting
1 egg white

For the icing
1 egg white
125g icing sugar
1 teaspoon rum

A classic combination of flavours, these tasty biscuits go perfectly with a cup of coffee, or a cup of tea if you prefer.

Nuss-Kaffee-Plätzchen
Walnut and Coffee Biscuits

MAKES ABOUT 60

1 egg
1 teaspoon instant coffee granules
100g unsalted butter, at room temperature
75g icing sugar
75g ground walnuts
60g plain flour, plus extra for dusting
1 pinch salt

To decorate
white chocolate
about 60 coffee beans

Break the egg into a small bowl and beat in the coffee until dissolved. Using an electric mixer and a separate bowl, cream the butter and sugar together. Beat in the coffee mixture, then add the walnuts, flour and salt. The dough will be quite soft. Cover with clingfilm and leave in the fridge for at least 2 hours.

Divide the chilled dough into 4 equal pieces for ease of handling. On a well-floured surface, use your hands to roll each piece into a log about 3cm in diameter. Cover with clingfilm and place in the freezer for at least 1 hour.

Once the dough has solidified enough to hold its shape, preheat the oven to 170°C fan/gas mark 5 and line 2 baking sheets with baking paper.

Take the dough out of the freezer, one piece at a time, and unwrap. Cut into 1cm slices and place them on the prepared baking sheets, spacing them at least 3cm apart, as these biscuits spread quite a bit. Bake for 11–14 minutes, until the edges start to darken. Set aside to cool on the sheets for a few minutes – they will be quite delicate – before transferring to a wire rack to cool completely.

Once the biscuits are cool, place the white chocolate in a heatproof bowl and microwave on High in 10-second bursts, stirring after each burst, until it is just runny enough to work with. Alternatively, you can use the bain-marie method (see page 16). Using a spoon, or a piping bag fitted with a 1.5cm round nozzle, place or pipe a little dollop of melted chocolate on each biscuit. Press a coffee bean into the chocolate and leave to set.

If stored in an airtight container, these biscuits will improve in flavour over the first 2 days, and will keep for at least 2 weeks.

The dough used in these biscuits is very similar to that used in Linzer Torte (see page 92), the classic Christmas cake made in my childhood home. Apart from being full of traditional spices, which makes them very delicious, these are quick and easy to make. A seasonal must-have.

Linzer Weihnachtsplätzchen
Linzer Christmas Biscuits

Sift the flour, cocoa powder, almonds, caster sugar and spices into a big bowl. Add the butter and rub it in.

Add the egg and the brandy (if using) and knead until the dough holds together. If you have time, cover it with clingfilm and leave to rest in the fridge for 1 hour.

Preheat the oven to 175°C fan/gas mark 6. Line 2 baking sheets with baking paper.

Take a piece of dough and roll it into a log 2cm in diameter. Cut the log into 2cm pieces and roll them into balls. Repeat until all dough is used up.

Push your index finger about two-thirds of the way into each ball of dough, then half-fill the holes with the jam. Transfer to the prepared sheets (the biscuits don't spread much while baking) and bake for 12–15 minutes.

Set aside to cool on the baking sheet for 10 minutes before transferring them to a wire rack to cool completely. Take care, as they are quite fragile while hot.

These biscuits taste great on the day they are baked, but their aroma and flavour are even better if stored for a week or longer in an airtight container. Dust with icing sugar to serve.

MAKES 50–60

240g plain flour
30g cocoa powder
200g ground almonds (skin on, if possible)
175g caster sugar
2 teaspoons ground cinnamon
½ teaspoon ground cloves
200g unsalted butter, cubed
1 egg
1 tablespoon raspberry brandy (optional)
200g red berry jam (raspberry, redcurrant, or a mixture)
icing sugar, for dusting

The patterns in these biscuits – whether checkerboard, spiral or marbled – always fascinated me as a child. This is a biscuit where you can use your imagination to create your own designs to make something special, stunning and sophisticated.

Schwarz-Weiß-Gebäck
Black and White Biscuits

MAKES AT LEAST 40

For the white dough
270g plain flour, plus extra for dusting
125g cold unsalted butter, cubed
125g caster sugar
1 pinch salt
zest of 1 lemon
1 teaspoon vanilla paste
2 tablespoons beaten egg, plus more if needed

For the black dough
240g plain flour, plus extra for dusting
125g cold unsalted butter, cubed
30g cocoa powder
125g caster sugar
1 pinch salt
2 tablespoons beaten egg, plus more if needed

For each dough, put all the ingredients into a bowl and mix by hand or with an electric mixer fitted with a paddle attachment. If the dough is too stiff, add a bit more egg or a little water. The dough should hold together nicely and feel smooth. Cover each bowl with clingfilm and leave to rest at room temperature for about 1 hour.

Note: When making these biscuits, it's best to start with small amounts of dough, to get a feel for the way it handles.

To make spiral biscuits: Weigh out equal amounts of each dough. On a lightly floured surface, roll each piece into a rectangle about 2mm thick.

Place 1 sheet of dough on top of the other and gently press down. Cut one of the 4 sides straight, then roll up your dough, starting at the straight side. Wrap in clingfilm and place in the fridge.

To make checkerboard biscuits: Weigh out equal amounts of each dough (don't use up all of it, as you'll need some more at the end). On a lightly floured surface, roll each piece into a rectangle about 9cm wide and 3mm thick; the length doesn't matter so much.

Place 1 sheet of dough on top of the other and gently press down. Trim the edges straight. Cut your rectangle into 3 lengthways strips, each about 3cm wide. Place the strips on top of each other so that there are 6 layers, with black and white dough alternating. Make sure the long edges are clean and straight. Carefully cut into lengthways slices about 3mm thick. Now rearrange those slices – without the layers separating – so that the white and black doughs also alternate on top to create a checkerboard pattern. Roll out a thin sheet of dough, wrap it around the checkerboard layers, then wrap tightly in clingfilm and place in the fridge.

To make marbled biscuits: Very briefly knead together your offcuts or leftover pieces of black and white dough to create a swirly ball. Roll this into a log about 3cm in diameter. Wrap in clingfilm and place in the fridge.

Once the various logs have chilled and are firm, take them out of the fridge. At this stage, you can also freeze the rolls of dough to use later.

Preheat the oven to 180°C fan/gas mark 6. Line 2 baking sheets with baking paper.

Without unwrapping them, cut the logs into slices about 4mm thick, or whatever your personal preference. Keeping the clingfilm on prevents the dough from falling apart while being sliced.

Carefully remove the clingfilm from each biscuit and place them on the prepared sheets, spacing them about 2cm apart. Bake for 8–10 minutes, then transfer to a wire rack to cool.

If stored in an airtight container, these biscuits will keep well for several weeks.

These are among my all-time favourites. During baking, the top of these biscuits rises up, so they appear to be standing on a pedestal (called a foot in Germany). Although characteristic, this foot sometimes refuses to develop, but the biscuits are delicious nonetheless. The surface of the baking sheet will, to some extent, determine the outcome, so you might need to experiment. Some old recipes say to rub the sheet with a beeswax candle, but I find that buttering the baking paper and dusting it with icing sugar works well. For best results, do not use the fan setting on your oven when baking these biscuits.

Anis-Plätzchen
Aniseed Biscuits

The night before you want to bake these biscuits, line a baking sheet with baking paper, then lightly grease with butter and dust with icing sugar.

Place the eggs and icing sugar in a bowl and whisk on high speed for about 20 minutes. Using a spoon, gently fold in the flour and aniseed.

Place cherry-sized amounts of the mixture on the prepared sheet, spacing them about 2cm apart. Set aside to stand uncovered in a cool place overnight. In the morning, the surface of them should be dry.

Preheat the oven to 200°C/gas mark 7 (see recipe introduction).

Bake the aniseed biscuits for 8–10 minutes, until light golden, and with any luck they should each have developed the characteristic foot. Set aside to cool, then store in an airtight container. The flavour will need some time to develop, but they will keep for at least 2 months.

MAKES ABOUT 60

butter, for greasing
3 eggs
225g icing sugar, plus extra for dusting
225g plain flour
1 teaspoon whole aniseed

Spritzen means 'to squirt', and that's exactly what is done with this biscuit dough. While a conventional piping bag is generally used, the dough can also be extruded from a meat mincer. This results in a rougher and larger surface area being exposed to the heat, yielding a different flavour and mouthfeel from the piped version.

The basic dough can be flavoured in different ways, such as the vanilla and variations included below, but feel free to experiment – perhaps with freeze-dried raspberries.

Spritzgebäck
Piped Biscuits

MAKES 8–60, DEPENDING ON SHAPE AND SIZE

175g unsalted butter, at room temperature
125g icing sugar
1 large egg
1 pinch salt
300g plain flour
1 tablespoon full-fat milk (optional)

For the flavourings (optional)
1 teaspoon vanilla bean paste
15g cocoa powder
1 teaspoon full-fat milk

For the filling or coating (optional)
1 quantity Dipping Chocolate, melted (see page 193)
jam of your preferred flavour
1 quantity Ganache (see page 85)

Preheat the oven to 160°C fan/gas mark 4. Line 2 baking sheets with baking paper.

Using an electric mixer, cream the butter and icing sugar together. Once soft and smooth, mix in the egg. Add the salt, then mix in the flour a bit at a time. If the resulting dough is very stiff, add the milk. The dough can now be flavoured as you wish.

To make vanilla biscuits: Take half the dough (about 250g) and work in the vanilla bean paste.

To make chocolate biscuits: Take half the dough (about 250g) and work in the cocoa powder and about another teaspoon of milk, to adjust the consistency.

The consistency of the dough required depends on how you are going to shape the biscuits. In Germany there are 2 traditional ways. You can get a biscuit maker attachment for your meat mincer. This allows you to make long strands of somewhat rough but not unattractive shapes, which are cut into pieces of about 6–10cm in length and shaped into rings, S-shapes, etc. The dough needs to be on the firm side for this.

If you want to pipe your biscuits, you will need a softer dough. Use a piping bag fitted with a medium star nozzle and pipe your shapes onto the prepared sheets. Among the classic shapes are dots, sticks, arches and hearts.

Bake your biscuits for 12–15 minutes. Vanilla biscuits should catch a just bit of colour on the edges. Set aside to cool before decorating.

These versatile biscuits can be eaten just as they are, or the ends can be dipped in melted chocolate. For something fancier, you can sandwich 2 of them together with jam or ganache, then dip them sideways in melted chocolate. Place on baking paper to set.

If stored in an airtight container, these biscuits keep very well for at least 4 weeks and actually improve in flavour over time.

These rum balls are ganache based, so the basic mixture can also be used to fill chocolates, truffles or macaroons.

BISCUITS

Rum-Kugeln
Rum Balls

Using an electric mixer, cream the butter and sugar together.

Place both types of chocolate in a heatproof bowl and microwave on High in 10-second bursts, stirring after each burst, until it has melted and is no warmer than 34°C. Be careful not to overheat it or the result will be grainy. Alternatively, you can use the bain-marie method (see page 16).

Add the chocolate and the ground cloves to the butter mixture and beat to combine. Once the ganache is smooth, keep mixing while adding the rum. Cover with clingfilm and place in the fridge for several hours, until fairly solid.

Set out 2 plates or shallow bowls. Cover the bottom of one with desiccated coconut and the other with cocoa powder. Also set out an empty plate for the finished rum balls.

Place a teaspoonful of the ganache between the palms of your hands and roll into a ball the size of a cherry. Roll the ball in either the coconut or cocoa powder, then transfer to the clean plate. I like to shape about 10 or so, then clean my hands before coating them.

Store the finished balls in an airtight container lined with kitchen paper and place in the fridge. They will keep for about 2 weeks.

MAKES ABOUT 60

200g unsalted butter, at room temperature
100g icing sugar
300g dark chocolate (50–70 per cent cocoa solids), broken into pieces
300g milk chocolate, broken into pieces
¼ teaspoon ground cloves
80g rum (ideally 80 per cent proof)

For coating
desiccated coconut
cocoa powder

Thanks to its nut content, the dough for these vanilla crescents is quite forgiving, by which I mean it remains pliable to shape without cracking. These biscuits are a favourite of my brother, and quite easy and quick to make. It wouldn't be Christmas without them.

Vanille-Gipfele
Vanilla Crescents

MAKES ABOUT 40

40g vanilla sugar (for homemade, see page 194) or 40g caster sugar and ½ teaspoon vanilla bean paste
120g unsalted butter, at room temperature
120g plain flour
80g ground almonds
1 teaspoon vanilla bean paste
100g icing sugar, for dusting

Preheat the oven to 170°C fan/gas mark 5. Line a baking sheet with baking paper.

Place all the ingredients, except the icing sugar, in a bowl and work the dough with your hands until smooth. Roll it into a log about 2cm thick, then slice it widthways into 2cm rounds. Roll each round between your hands to create a mini log tapered at each end. Place on the prepared sheet and bend the tapered ends inward to get a crescent shape. Make more crescents in the same way, spacing them about 2cm apart.

Bake for about 10 minutes, until still pale but starting to firm up. Set aside to cool on the sheet for about 3 minutes, then gently transfer to a wire rack. Once cool, dust the crescents with icing sugar.

If stored in an airtight container, these biscuits will keep for at least 6 weeks.

These biscuits offer a warm, comforting melt-in-the-mouth feel with a lovely balance of orange and pistachio.

Pistazien-Plätzchen
Pistachio and Orange Biscuits

Using an electric mixer, cream the butter and sugar together. Mix in the egg and orange zest, then add the salt, flour, pistachios, mixed peel and vanilla paste, and mix again. The dough will be quite soft. Cover with clingfilm and leave in the fridge for at least 2 hours

Divide the chilled dough into 4 equal pieces. On a well-floured surface, use your hands to roll each piece into a log about 3cm in diameter. Wrap each with clingfilm and place in the freezer for at least 1 hour.

When the dough has solidified enough to hold its shape, preheat the oven to 170°C fan/gas mark 5 and line 2 baking sheets with baking paper.

Take the dough out of the freezer, one piece at a time, and unwrap. Cut into 1cm slices and place on the prepared sheets, spacing them at least 3cm apart as these biscuits spread quite a bit in the oven. Bake for 11–14 minutes, until the edges of the biscuits darken.

Set aside to cool on the baking sheet for a few minutes – they will be quite delicate – before transferring to a wire rack to cool completely.

Once the biscuits are cool, prepare the icing. Sift the icing sugar into a bowl. Add the orange juice bit by bit, stirring constantly, until the mixture runs off a fork in thin strands, but will stay on your biscuits. Drizzle the biscuits with icing in a random pattern. Leave to set.

If stored in an airtight container, these biscuits will improve in flavour over the first 2 days, and will keep for at least 2 weeks.

MAKES ABOUT 60

100g unsalted butter, at room temperature
65g icing sugar
1 egg
zest of 1 orange
1 pinch salt
60g plain flour, plus extra for dusting
75g ground pistachios (green)
75g mixed peel
½ teaspoon vanilla bean paste

For the icing
50g icing sugar
about 2 teaspoons orange juice

The dots of jam peeping through this biscuit sometimes give it the appearance of a cheeky face, hence some of its other names – *Spitzbuben* (rascals) and *Linzer Augen* (eyes). The name *Hilda-Brötle* (little Hilda breads) comes from Princess Hilda of Nassau, the last Grand Duchess of Baden, who is said to have loved them and baked them herself.

Hilda-Brötle

MAKES 30–50,
DEPENDING ON CUTTER SIZE

150g unsalted butter, cubed
50g caster sugar
1 egg yolk
1 pinch salt
10g vanilla sugar (for homemade, see page 194)
250g plain flour, plus extra for dusting
icing sugar, for dusting
200g seedless jam (raspberry, redcurrant or similar)
1 tablespoon water

Preheat the oven to 160°C fan/gas mark 4. Line a baking sheet with baking paper.

Using an electric mixer, cream the butter and sugar together. Whisk in the egg yolk, salt and vanilla sugar. Sift in the flour, then use your hands to form a smooth, pliable dough.

On a lightly floured work surface, roll out the dough until 3mm thick. Using fluted cutters 6–8cm in diameter, stamp out as many circles as you like. Transfer them to the prepared sheet, spacing them 2cm apart. Using a 2–3cm cutter – a big piping nozzle or the screw cap of a bottle work well – stamp out and remove the centre of half the biscuits.

Bake for about 10 minutes, until light golden. Transfer to a wire rack and leave to cool.

Once cool, place the biscuits with a hole precisely on top of the full biscuits. Dust with icing sugar.

Put the jam into a saucepan, add the water and bring to the boil, stirring. Using a spoon, carefully pour hot jam into the holes in the biscuits. Leave to cool, then store in an airtight container. These will keep for at least 4 weeks.

Pretzels, sweet and savoury, have been around for over a thousand years, and they have long been a symbol of the baking trade in Germany. Making pretzels as small as these can be a bit fiddly, but the results are very rewarding, and they are great as a special gift.

Schoko-Brezeln
Chocolate Pretzels

Preheat the oven to 180°C fan/gas mark 6. Line 2 baking trays with baking paper.

Combine the flour, salt and spices in a bowl, then rub in the cubed butter. Add the sugar, rum, water and egg yolk, and mix until a dough forms and holds together. This dough needs some gluten development to allow shaping, so knead it (by hand or in a mixer fitted with a dough hook) until it becomes smooth and stretchy. This will take about 5 minutes. Set aside to rest for 10 minutes.

Cut the dough into pieces the size of a walnut. On a lightly dusted work surface, gently roll a piece of dough into a thin strand about 30cm in length. Try not to tear the dough; if it resists being rolled out, let it rest for a few minutes and work on another piece.

Shape the strand into a pretzel (see photo opposite) and place on a prepared baking sheet. Repeat with the remaining dough pieces, spacing them about 2cm apart.

Bake for about 12 minutes, until the tips are lightly browned. Transfer to a wire rack and leave to cool completely.

Dip the pretzels in the melted chocolate, coating them completely. Let the excess drip off, then place the pretzels on a sheet of baking paper to set.

If stored in an airtight container in a cool place, these pretzels will keep for at least 2 weeks.

MAKES ABOUT 30

225g strong white flour, plus extra for dusting
½ teaspoon salt
1 teaspoon ground cinnamon
¼ teaspoon ground allspice
70g cold unsalted butter, cubed
70g caster sugar
50g rum
40ml water
1 egg yolk
1 quantity Dipping Chocolate (see page 193)

BISCUITS

Marzipan has long been used as a modelling material to make all sorts of fruits and vegetables. Using it to model potatoes might strike you as an unusual choice, but marzipan potatoes are as much a part of Christmas in Germany as cinnamon stars and Lebkuchen. In our family, marzipan potatoes were a popular gift, packed in little cellophane bags alongside our other presents. They are as traditional in Germany as the tangerine in the toe of a Christmas stocking is in Britain.

Marzipankartoffeln
Marzipan Potatoes

MAKES ABOUT 60

200g homemade Marzipan (see page 192, or use ready-made)
125g icing sugar, sifted, plus extra for dusting
1 tablespoon almond liqueur
cocoa powder, for dusting

Soften the marzipan by kneading it. If it gets too sticky, dust the work surface with icing sugar.

Break the marzipan into small pieces and place in a large bowl. Add the icing sugar and the liqueur and knead again until the marzipan mixture is smooth and pliable. Depending on its age/composition, you might need to add more icing sugar or some water to achieve the desired consistency.

Break cherry-sized pieces off the kneaded marzipan and roll them into balls. Prick them a few times with a cocktail stick to emulate the black dots on a potato.

Roll the balls in the cocoa powder, then dust them off until they remind you of irregularly coloured potatoes.

Lebkuchen are classified according to their ratios of flour, egg, sugar and nuts. The less flour they contain, the more special they are – less flour means more of the expensive ingredients, like fruit and nuts. Being moist, these are best baked on rice paper or *Back Oblaten* (German baking wafers) – as described on page 15 – so these are classified as Oblaten Lebkuchen, a really indulgent treat. You can cover them in chocolate or with *Fadenzuckerglasur*, a type of hot sugar glaze that is traditionally used for Lebkuchen.

TIP:

If you bake the Lebkuchen on baking paper rather than *Back Oblaten* or rice paper, apply the hot sugar glaze or dipping chocolate all over and set aside to cool completely before attempting to remove them from the sheets.

Feine Lebkuchen
Special Gingerbread

Preheat the oven to 190°C fan/gas mark 6½. Line 2 baking sheets with baking paper or preferably 30 *Back Oblaten* (large round German baking wafers, 7cm in diameter), or 2 large sheets of rice paper (there is no need to cut the rice paper into circles, as it will tear roughly into shape when the baked Lebkuchen are lifted off at the end, and you can trim off any untidy bits before glazing).

Blend the ground almonds and icing sugar in a blender or food processor until lumps form. Add 1 egg white and continue blending until smooth.

Transfer the almond mixture to a bowl, add the brown sugar and mix by hand until smooth. Add the remaining egg whites bit by bit and continue to mix until they are fully incorporated. Stir in the mixed peel, hazelnuts, flour and spice.

Place spoonfuls of the batter on the prepared sheets, spacing them 4cm apart; alternatively, use a piping bag fitted with a large round nozzle to pipe shapes instead. It is traditional for this kind of Lebkuchen to be made in circles 7cm wide.

Bake for about 12 minutes, until the edges are lightly brown.

Meanwhile, if you want to glaze the biscuits with sugar glaze, place the glaze ingredients in a saucepan a few minutes before the Lebkuchen are ready, and bring to the boil. Once the mixture reaches 109°C on a sugar thermometer, take it off the heat. Brush the hot glaze immediately over just the top of the Lebkuchen and set aside to cool on the baking sheets.

If you are covering the Lebkuchen in chocolate, let the biscuits cool completely first. Then use a brush to coat the top and sides of the biscuits, or dip them carefully into the melted chocolate. Set aside to cool.

If stored in an airtight container, these Lebkuchen improve a lot over time and keep for at least 4 weeks.

MAKES ABOUT 30

125g ground almonds
125g icing sugar
4 egg whites
300g brown sugar
80g mixed peel
100g ground hazelnuts
100g plain flour
1 tablespoon Gingerbread Spice (see page 195)
1 quantity Dipping Chocolate (optional, see page 193)

For the sugar glaze (optional)
250g sugar
100ml water

There are many varieties of Lebkuchen in Germany, most of which are also produced commercially. These commercial recipes are usually a closely guarded secret and often involve special doughs that take months to mature before they can be baked. My family, like many others, enjoyed the ease of buying – or being gifted – exquisite Lebkuchen, especially the jam-filled hearts. However, these biscuits are easier to make than it seems, so don't be afraid to give them a try.

Gefüllte Lebkuchen-Herzen
Filled Gingerbread Hearts

Using a large spoon or a spatula, mix the flours, egg, honey and spice in a large bowl, then knead until a smooth dough forms. Cover with clingfilm and set aside to rest for at least 1 hour at room temperature; even better is to leave it overnight in the fridge.

Preheat the oven to 170°C fan/gas mark 5. Line 2 baking sheets with baking paper.

Once the dough has rested, mix the rum and baking ammonia in a small bowl, then knead this into the dough. Transfer to a lightly floured work surface and roll out the dough until 6mm thick.

Stamp out the biscuits using a heart-shaped cutter 4–6cm wide. Transfer half the hearts to the baking sheets, then use a teaspoon to place some jam on them – the amount depends on the size of your hearts, but it is important that it doesn't spill over the edge. Place a second heart biscuit on top of the jam and seal it by carefully pushing the edge of the upper heart down towards the baking sheet, creating a well-rounded edge.

Bake for 12–15 minutes. The biscuits should be lightly browned and a bit soft. Set aside to cool completely. Once cool, cover the Lebkuchen with the chocolate and leave to set.

Stored in a cool place, these biscuits will develop an intense flavour over time, so try to leave them for at least 3 days before eating. They will keep for several weeks.

MAKES ABOUT 20

300g strong white flour, plus extra for dusting
100g wholemeal wheat flour
100g wholemeal rye flour
1 egg
400g honey
4 teaspoons Gingerbread Spice (see page 195)
4 teaspoons rum
2 teaspoons baking ammonia (see page 59) or bicarbonate of soda
apricot or plum jam, as needed
1 quantity Dipping Chocolate (see page 193)

I believe Hansel and Gretel would have liked some of these Lebkuchen! They use a 'starter' made by allowing flour and honey to mature together. Although these ingredients create very little fermentation, if any at all, they do develop a special flavour and texture provided they sit for at least three weeks. Some bakeries let their starter rest for up to seven months!

These Lebkuchen keep very well for weeks while improving in flavour, making them ideal presents. They're also a perfect teatime snack to have in winter, so it's just as well that this recipe makes quite a large batch.

Honig-Lebkuchen
Honey Gingerbread

MAKES 40–100,
DEPENDING ON SIZE

For the starter
200g plain flour, plus extra for dusting
150g white or wholemeal spelt flour
150g light or wholemeal rye flour
400g honey

For the Lebkuchen
2 tablespoons Gingerbread Spice (see 195)
1 teaspoon bicarbonate of soda
1 teaspoon baking ammonia (see page 59) or baking powder
1 egg
80g ground almonds
100g mixed peel
blanched almonds, as needed
glacé cherries, as needed
2 egg whites, lightly beaten, for glazing

Combine the starter ingredients in a bowl and mix or knead until a ball of dough forms. Transfer to an airtight container or wrap it in clingfilm and store in a cool place for at least 1 week, or up to 3 months.

Preheat the oven to 180°C fan/gas mark 6. Line 2 baking sheets with baking paper.

Put all of the starter into a large bowl and break it into little pieces. Add the spice, bicarbonate of soda and baking ammonia/powder, the egg, ground almonds and mixed peel. Mix thoroughly until well combined and the dough feels smooth.

On a lightly floured work surface, roll out the dough until 6mm thick. Cut into rectangles 6 x 4cm, or stamp out circles using a 5cm cutter. Transfer to the prepared sheets, spacing them about 3cm apart. Decorate by pushing blanched almonds and glacé cherry halves into the dough. A traditional pattern would be 4 almonds near the corners of the rectangle, and a cherry half in the middle. Bake for 12 minutes.

Remove from the oven and immediately use a pastry brush to glaze the biscuits with a thin coat of egg white. Set aside to dry and cool.

If stored in an airtight container, these Lebkuchen will keep for at least 8 weeks and are great as gifts.

My grandma Margarethe's family came from Eisenach in Thuringia, and with them came culinary traditions that were very different from those in the Black Forest region where I grew up. Every Christmas she made a batch of savoury cheese biscuits, which had a special place among all the traditional sweet things.

Käseplätzchen
Cheese Biscuits

Place the butter in a bowl with the flour and rub together with your fingers. Mix in the egg, cheese and caraway seeds, then knead with your hands until a smooth dough forms. Cover in clingfilm and leave to rest in the fridge for about 1 hour.

Preheat the oven to 180°C fan/gas mark 6. Line 2 baking sheets with baking paper.

Lightly flour a work surface. Roll out the dough until 6mm thick. Using small cutters, stamp out your favourite shapes, then transfer them to the prepared sheets. Bake for about 14 minutes, or until the edges become golden brown. Set aside to cool on the sheets, then store in an airtight container. They will keep for about 4 weeks.

MAKES ABOUT
60 SMALL BISCUITS

125g cold unsalted butter, cubed
125g plain flour, plus extra for dusting
1 egg
100g strong cheese (such as mature Cheddar) grated
1 tablespoon caraway seeds, lightly crushed

My aunt Olga made these for my grandmother every year, using festive embossed moulds or stamps, and I was always intrigued by the clarity of the impressed designs. Springerle require patience, so don't cut corners when whisking the eggs or drying the biscuits overnight, otherwise they will be dense and won't develop the typical 'feet' (see page 33).

Special Springerle moulds are often hand-carved from fine-grained cherry wood and can be bought online or at Christmas markets. The variety of motifs is impressive, ranging from Christmas ornaments to cartoon characters. Make sure to buy moulds that are designed for baking, not those that are meant to be purely decorative.

Springerle

MAKES 15–20 LARGE SPRINGERLE

4 large eggs
500g icing sugar
¼ teaspoon baking ammonia or
  ½ teaspoon bicarbonate of soda
2 teaspoons rum
500g plain flour, plus extra for dusting
zest of 1 lemon
20g aniseed
cornflour, for dusting (optional)

Using an electric mixer, whisk the eggs on high speed, then add the icing sugar bit by bit. Once all the sugar has been added, continue whisking at high speed for about 20 minutes.

Dissolve the baking ammonia in the rum. If you're using bicarbonate of soda instead, add it with the flour in the next step.

Once the egg mixture is ready, fold in the flour and lemon zest, then add the rum mixture to the bowl. The aniseed can be added at this stage, or you can sprinkle it on the baking sheet later and place the springerle on top (this gives a cleaner result).

Cover with clingfilm and set the dough aside to rest at room temperature for about 1 hour. It should be less sticky after that.

Set out 2 baking sheets and line with baking paper. Sprinkle the aniseed over the sheets, if you haven't added it to the dough already.

RAISING AGENTS FOR BISCUITS

Baking ammonia (ammonium hydrogen carbonate) is the raising ingredient used in many German biscuits that have to sit for at least 12 hours before being baked (Springerle and Lebkuchen, for example). That's because it releases its gases only when subjected to heat, so can survive the wait when making Springerle. You can buy it online in the UK.

Bicarbonate of soda (sodium bicarbonate) releases its gas when brought into contact with an acid ingredient (such as lemon juice, for example) and subjected to heat. It will make the dough softer, so is not ideal for Springerle or other biscuits that need to keep their shape.

Baking powder (sodium bicarbonate plus an acid, such as cream of tartar) creates gas immediately it comes into contact with moisture. It therefore loses some of its raising potential before it even reaches the oven if the dough is left to stand for too long.

Roll out the dough on a lightly floured work surface until 1cm thick. If necessary, lightly dust the surface of the rolled dough with cornflour to prevent sticking, then apply the moulds or stamps to it. Using a small, sharp knife, cut neatly around each design, then transfer the biscuits to the prepared baking sheets. Set aside, uncovered, to dry overnight in a cool place.

Preheat the oven to 140°C fan/gas mark 3.

Bake the biscuits for 20–30 minutes. The surface should still be white and the designs clearly visible, but the biscuits should have risen and be supported by the characteristic pedestal foot. At this point they should still be a bit soft. Set aside to cool on the baking sheets.

Although delicious to eat straight away, Springerle are best stored in an airtight container and left for about 3 weeks before being eaten.

Building and decorating this gingerbread house, designed in the style of a traditional Black Forest farmhouse, might seem a little daunting, but with the help of the templates provided, some well-baked gingerbread and a bit of patience it should be great fun and yield impressive results.

The southern part of the Black Forest is mountainous, and used to be a fairly poor region of Germany because there wasn't much land suitable for growing crops. Farming was therefore centred around forestry and livestock, such as cattle, pigs, sheep, goats and chickens, but harsh winters and deep snow made life very difficult. The traditional Black Forest farmhouse was designed to cope with these conditions, and everything needed to get through the winter was under one huge roof.

At the back of the house is storage space for hay, grains and vegetables, usually accessible through a big barn door. To the front are stables for the animals, and alongside, or sometimes above the stables, are the family's living quarters, usually heated by a central wood-burning stove. The proximity of the animals also added some warmth. I remember visiting friends of my grandpa in houses like this. We sat in the kitchen, which was open to the rafters, and smoke from the stove was channelled up to them. There, among the blackened timbers, hung sides of *Speck* (ham) and sausages being preserved by the smoke.

Thanks to the roof's long overhangs, a generous area around the building was protected from the elements, and farmers were able to access their stores and care for their animals without having to wade through the snow. There were always lots of things to see in the yards of these farmhouses – piles of firewood, tools, wagon wheels, fences...

All these things can be modelled from the same gingerbread dough as the house, so be creative when decorating the exterior. If you like, you can also add some marzipan people.

Based on Scandinavian recipes, this gingerbread holds up very well. The use of margarine and baking ammonia (see page 59) further increases the durability of the gingerbread, and the dough spreads very little when baked. For best results, place the templates on the gingerbread while still hot and soft and trim the shapes to size, then transfer them to a wire rack to cool. Once you start assembling your gingerbread house, the shapes can be easily adjusted further using a fine grater or a clean woodworking file.

The dough will keep in the fridge for up to four days, which is very useful as your construction project will take a bit of time – allow a total of about 10 hours to bake, assemble and decorate the house. You can keep things simpler, if you like, by giving your farmhouse a plain roof, instead of the tiered thatched roof shown in the photograph on the following pages. Any leftover dough can be made into gingerbread biscuits.

You can download a PDF of the templates for this gingerbread house, designed to print at the correct size on A4 paper, via the QR code below:

Lebkuchenhaus
Gingerbread House

Place the margarine, butter, sugar, honey and milk in a saucepan and heat until the fats have melted. Set aside to cool.

Sift the flour, baking ammonia and spice into a bowl.

Pour the milk mixture into another large bowl, then stir in the spiced flour a bit at a time. The resulting dough will be very sticky. Wrap it in clingfilm, or simply cover the bowl, and let it rest in the fridge for at least 2 hours. The dough is now workable.

Preheat the oven to 180°C fan/gas mark 6.

Roll out portions of the dough on a lightly floured work surface, making them 4mm thick for large parts, such as the roof and walls, and 3mm thick for the balustrade and other small parts. Use the templates (see opposite and pages 70–71) to cut out the shapes of the building and transfer them to lined baking sheets. If preferred, you can roll out the dough on sheets of baking paper or silicone baking mats, then cut around the templates on those surfaces so that you can lift the shapes easily onto baking sheets or into the oven without the risk of distorting them. Before you bake them, check the dimensions of all the parts and pull them gently back to size if needed.

For the perforated balustrade, you can stamp out your preferred decorative holes using little cookie cutters. You can also use the blunt edge of a knife blade to emboss lines on the walls in order to create the look of wooden slats.

It looks nice to have a gingerbread house with a door that's ajar, so remove the cut-out part on the template completely and bake it separately. [A]. Bake the barn door separately from its wall too, in 2 halves, as indicated on the template [B]. Fill the window openings evenly with crushed boiled sweets before baking.

continues on page 66

MAKES 1

For the gingerbread
170g margarine
170g unsalted butter
300g caster sugar
420g honey
150ml full-fat milk
1110g strong white flour, plus extra for dusting
2 teaspoons baking ammonia (see page 59) or bicarbonate of soda
2 tablespoons Gingerbread Spice (see page 195)
boiled sweets, crushed, for the windowpanes

For the royal icing
70g pasteurized egg whites
400g icing sugar, sifted, plus extra if needed and for dusting
lemon juice
food colouring, as desired

For the marzipan figures
marzipan, about 85g per figure (for homemade, see page 192, or use ready-made)
cocoa powder
food colourings of your choice
1 quantity Royal Icing (see above)
chocolate, melted, as needed
pasteurized egg white

Bake the larger parts of the structure for about 14 minutes, and the smaller ones for 8–12 minutes. Keep an eye on the small pieces so they don't get burnt. As ovens vary, do make sure all the pieces are baked through – they should not bend when cool. If need be, return them to the oven for a few more minutes.

If you want to add a thatched roof, roll out the remaining dough very thinly (2mm) on a sheet of baking paper to a rectangle of about 30 x 20cm. Cut the dough in strips about 6cm wide. You will need around 10 of these strips to cover the whole roof – use the templates for the large roof parts [G and H] and the two roof triangles [I and J] as a rough guide for the lengths. You can trim the ends of the strips to size later, when you assemble the house. Space the strips about 1cm apart on the baking paper, making sure they are still straight after you've moved them into place. To create the look of straw, use the blunt edge of a knife blade to emboss the strips with tightly spaced, slightly irregular parallel lines.

For the royal icing
If assembling the gingerbread house with children helping you, it is safer to use royal icing as your glue rather than isomalt because isomalt has to be heated to a very high temperature. Another advantage of icing is that it can be made in advance and stored in the fridge until needed. Isomalt, on the other hand, has to be melted just before starting the assembly, and needs to be reheated if it cools and gets too stiff to work with. Take care not to overheat it, as it can become a bit dark. Whichever glue you opt for, do make sure to give everything enough time to set before proceeding to the next step.

Whisk the egg whites in a bowl until they are light and frothy. Fold in the icing sugar bit by bit.

Add a few drops of lemon juice and whisk the icing until it is stiff and bright white. Adjust the consistency as necessary with additional lemon juice or icing sugar. Piping work requires slightly stiff icing, while flooding needs something more liquid. Add food colouring as you wish.

To assemble the house
You will need a cake board big enough to hold the house with its surroundings – about 30 x 21cm should be fine (the size of an A4 sheet of paper). A piece of plywood covered in foil works well.

Make sure you have baked all the pieces required, and that they are hard and dry. Check the dimensions of your pieces against the templates and adjust them if necessary, using a fine grater or file to shave the sides as needed.

Mark the position of the 2 side walls [A and B] and the 2 inner supporting walls [C and D] on your base. Check again that the 2 inner walls are exactly the same size, filing them if necessary.

Using royal icing or isomalt, glue the back wall [E] and 1 side wall [A] onto the base. Don't forget to apply glue to the corner of the house, where the 2 walls meet. Use a triangular ruler or a piece of firm card with a right angle to make sure the walls are upright and meet each other in a right angle.

Glue the inner supporting walls [C and D] to the base and the side wall. Add the missing side wall [B] and the front of the house [F].

Make sure the large roof parts [G and H] are exactly the size of the template, filing them to match if necessary. Before gluing, check the fit of the left roof panel on the house. The 2 top corners of it should meet the points of the inner supporting walls, and the front and back edges should meet the corners of the house as indicated. If necessary, shave off some of the side wall at an angle to get a good fit. Glue the left roof panel to the house. Do the same for the right roof panel.

Fit the small roof triangle [I] to the front and glue it in place, then do the same for the large roof triangle [J] at the back.

Fit the floor of the balcony [K] to the front of the house, just below the level of the top row of windows. Add the balustrade [L].

If you are adding the thatched roof, sprinkle the strips for the roof lightly with icing sugar and rub it into the ridged pattern. Glue the strips onto the roof, starting at the bottom edge. Let the strips overlap lightly. Complete one side of the roof and trim the thatch before moving on to the other side. Finish by adding strips to the roof triangles at the front and back.

Use the remaining icing to pipe snow, icicles and decorative outlines on the finished house.

continues overleaf

For the marzipan figurines
Santa, snowmen, logs and children are decorative additions to your gingerbread landscape. The method given below is for a generic figure to which you can add hair, beards, clothing and hats of whatever style you like. Note: When working with marzipan, it's important to keep your hands and work surface clean.

Divide 85g marzipan into 3 pieces: 15g for the head, 40g for the body and limbs, and 30g for extras, such as hair and items of clothing.

Dip a cocktail stick into the cocoa powder or food colouring and add it to the marzipan for the head. Work it in with your fingers, adding more if necessary to achieve the effect you want. Take about two-thirds of the head marzipan (reserving the remainder for the neck) and roll it into a ball. Using a modelling tool or skewer, create 2 indents for the eyes, and mark the mouth if you wish (many marzipan figures look fine without a mouth, but you can roll a very thin strand of pink marzipan to use as lips if you like). Pipe a small amount of royal icing into the eye indents. When set, pipe a dot of chocolate onto the eyeballs to mark the irises.

Tint the body marzipan in the colour(s) you want – make the body all red for a Santa figurine, or divide it in half and perhaps make a figure with a blue top and green trousers, for example. Shape the body piece(s) as you wish, then colour and shape the figure's various clothes and accessories, such as the hat, shoes and belt.

Assemble your marzipan figurine, using a small paintbrush to apply tiny dabs of egg white as glue. Let each joint dry before tackling the next one.

TIP:

It's a good idea to check the size and fit of your paper templates (see overleaf and page 62) by sticking the pieces together with masking tape – if the paper house comes together well, so will your gingerbread house.

FLOOR PLAN

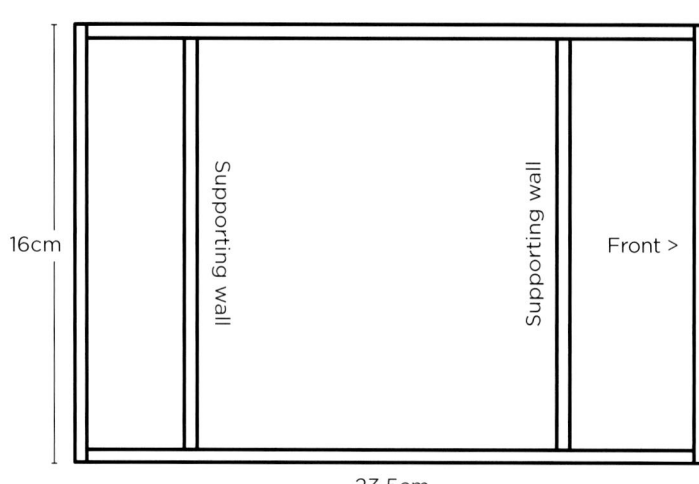

A LEFT WALL

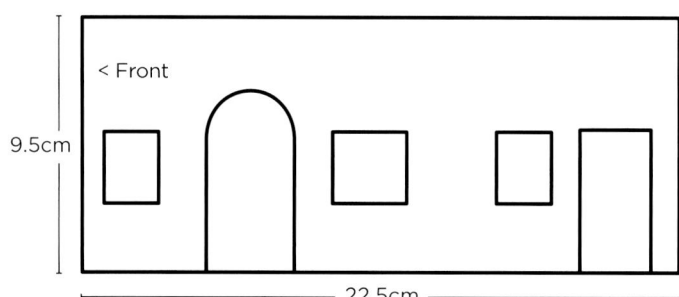

B RIGHT WALL

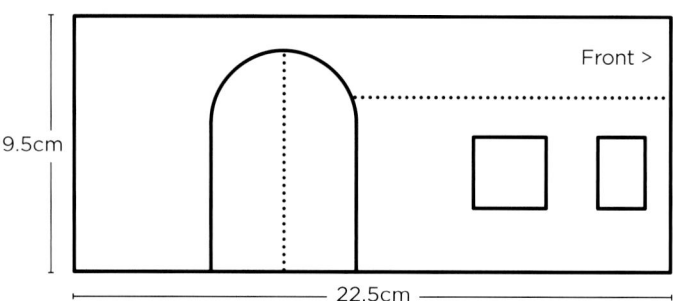

C & D SUPPORTING WALL X2

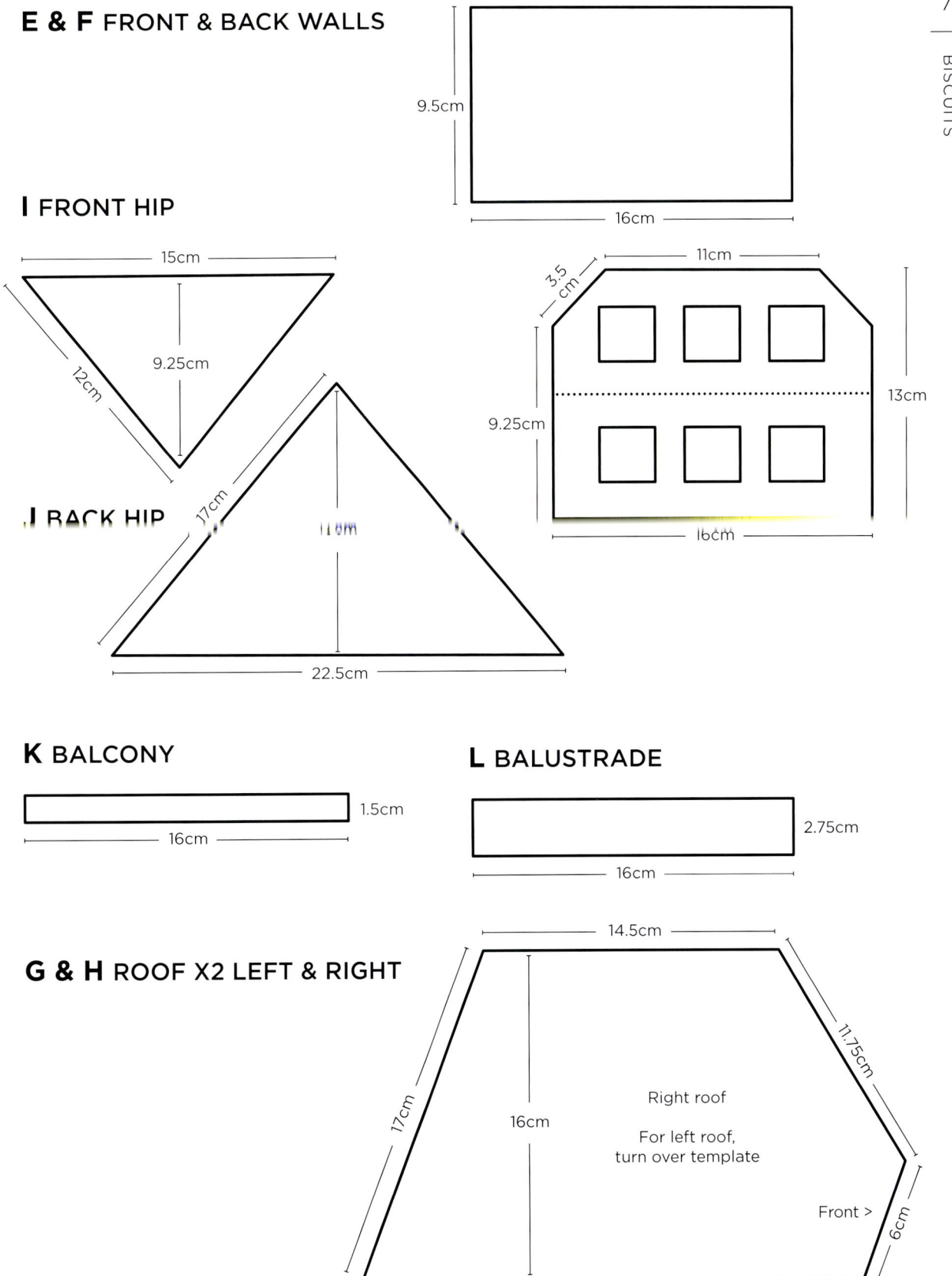

Advent as a musician

While I was at university studying physics, I rediscovered my passion for playing music and started taking recorder lessons again. I also attended courses for amateur musicians, where I was soon playing double reeds or shawms (a precursor of the oboe, of Middle Eastern origin) and sackbut (an early version of the trombone that dates back to the fifteenth century). I made friends with other musicians, some of whom had connections to churches and other musical institutions. Around Christmas, we would meet up to spend time playing and singing together.

There were some memorable musical gatherings. The first time I was invited to attend one of these events, I spent a few days after Christmas with the family of a teacher and choir leader near Minden in North Rhine-Westphalia, along with musical friends from all over the place. There were about ten of us, all amateur multi-instrumentalists and singers. For three days, we sang and played our way through Heinrich Schütz's 'Geistliche Chormusik', a collection of motets from 1648. Playing Schütz's works on sackbut next to singers was an eye opener – it revealed to me how intricately text and musical expression can be interwoven, and how to express it on an instrument. We also played dance music by William Brade, an English composer of the early Baroque era, for which one of the musicians brought along a huge box of recorders of all sizes – I very much enjoyed playing the two-meter-tall bass recorder in C for those dance music sessions.

Eventually I was asked to play trombone in Schütz's version of the Christmas story, in which different instruments accompany the various characters: trumpets for Herod, violins for the angels, recorders for the shepherds and trombones for the high priests. I had the opportunity to perform this beautiful piece several times. When I decided to pursue early music in more depth, I found an incredibly kind and helpful teacher and for the next few years, Christmastime was very busy for me, filled with musical events.

If you could use a break from cooking, why not chill out with Schütz's Christmas Story? You can find versions of it on YouTube.

Bedtime for my brother and me.

Christmas at my grandparents, with my 'Oma' Ida and my cousins.

Cakes and Tarts

Glühwein-Kuchen
Mulled Wine Cake 78

Baumkuchen-Torte
Tree Cake 81

Jürgens Orange Bûche de Noël
Jürgen's Orange Yule Log 84

Weihnachts-Apfelkuchen
Christmas Apple Pie 89

Weihnachts-Linzertorte
Christmas Linzer Torte 93

Honigkuchen
Honey Cake or Lekach 94

Früchtekuchen mit Zimt im Glas
Cinnamon Fruit Cake in a Jar 97

First of all, I need to tell you that there are no German Christmas cakes or tarts as such – the traditional German bakes for this time of year are Christmas biscuits and stollen, neither of which are cakes. However, many traditional German cake recipes have been modified over time to give them a seasonal feel, often by adding spices or ingredients such as oranges or preserved fruit, making these cakes richer and more festive.

And then, while it might seem obvious and intuitive to translate the German word Kuchen as cake, and Torte as tart, things are not quite as straightforward as that. A German Torte is an elaborate type of cake, usually with a substantial amount of cream filling. A Kuchen is anything that is not a Torte. It can be made with sponge or shortcrust pastry, and it can be plain or filled. Examples include marble cake, Bundt cakes and Swiss rolls, but also traybakes and a type of bake that, in the UK, would be called a tart or a pie.

Finally, there are potentially confusing traditions in naming: a Linzer Torte would be classified as a Kuchen in Germany, and a tart in Britain.

Much easier and more enjoyable than trying to sort out these confusing names is to actually get baking, so let's get started!

In Germany, Christmas markets start on the Friday before the first Sunday in Advent, which is usually in late November, and last until 24 December. This means the weather can be very cold, so it's a great time to indulge in Glühwein (see page 186) with its characteristic spices. Those same spices, along with a dash of red wine, are used to flavour this cake. Like a mug of mulled wine, this cake has a warming and comforting quality.

Glühwein-Kuchen
Mulled Wine Cake

MAKES 1 X 26CM BUNDT CAKE

300g plain flour, plus extra for dusting
16g baking powder
1½ teaspoons ground cinnamon
¼ teaspoon ground cloves
¼ teaspoon ground star anise
⅛ teaspoon ground nutmeg
¼ teaspoon ground allspice
25g cocoa powder
225g caster sugar
20g vanilla sugar (for homemade, see page 194)
¼ teaspoon salt
275g unsalted butter, at room temperature, plus extra for greasing
4 large eggs
zest of 1 lemon
200ml fruity red wine
80g mixed peel

For the glaze
200g icing sugar
1 teaspoon lemon juice
about 3 tablespoons red wine

Preheat the oven to 175°C fan/gas mark 6. Butter a 26cm bundt tin, getting into all the crevices, and dust with flour.

Put the flour, baking powder, spices and cocoa powder into a bowl and mix to combine.

Put the caster sugar, vanilla sugar, salt and butter into a separate bowl and cream together using an electric mixer. Add the eggs and lemon zest and mix until everything is well incorporated. While continuing to mix, work in small amounts of the wine and the flour mixture, adding them alternately. Finally, stir in the mixed peel.

Pour the batter into the prepared tin and bake for about 1 hour. The cake is ready if it's separating from the tin and a skewer inserted into the thickest part comes out clean. Switch off the heat and let the cake cool inside the oven with the door held slightly ajar by a wooden spoon or a rolled-up tea towel. After 30 minutes, take the cake out of the oven and carefully remove it from the tin. Set aside on a wire rack to cool completely.

To make the glaze, sift the icing sugar into a bowl. Stir in the lemon juice, then add the wine a bit at a time, stirring constantly until the mixture is pourable but not runny. Pour the glaze over the cold cake – this can nicely enhance the pattern from your bundt tin. If stored in an airtight container, the cake will keep for about 1 week.

Baumkuchen gets its name from its appearance. Traditional bakeries make this cake by brushing the batter onto a large pole that rotates in front of an open fire or other heat source. Each layer is barbecued until it is golden brown, then the next layer of batter is brushed on. This results in a very long cake that looks a bit like a log, and slices of it display a pattern of the browned layers that look just like the growth rings of a tree.

The traditional method of making Baumkuchen requires special equipment and skill, but making it in a cake tin instead yields excellent results. But because this version is flat, it's called Baumkuchen-Torte or Schicht-Torte, rather than simply Baumkuchen. You can scale this recipe to suit a wide variety of cake tins – see the table below.

HOW MUCH BATTER?

Here's an easy way to scale the recipe to your tin size. If using an 18cm springform tin, for example, make 1.3 times the amount of the mixture above.

Metric size	Imperial size	Batter quantity
18 x 11cm	7 x 4½in	1
15 x 8cm	5¾ x 3¼in	0.6
20 x 10cm	8 x 4in	1
22 x 11cm	8½ x 4½in	1.2
23 x 13cm	9 x 5in	1.5
18cm diameter	7in diameter	1.3
21cm diameter	8in diameter	1.7
23cm diameter	9in diameter	2.1
25cm diameter	10in diameter	2.5

Baumkuchen-Torte
Tree Cake

Grease an 18 x 11cm loaf tin and line the base with baking paper.

Place the egg whites and salt in a large bowl and whisk into soft peaks. While continuing to whisk, add 70g of the caster sugar bit by bit. Continue whisking until a smooth, shiny meringue forms. Set aside.

Using an electric mixer, cream the butter and remaining 75g of the caster sugar together. Mix in the egg yolks one at a time, until they are completely incorporated, then add the vanilla bean paste.

Sift the cornflour, plain flour and baking powder into a separate bowl, then add to the butter mixture a bit at a time, folding in each addition before adding the next. Now carefully fold in the meringue.

Heat the grill until red hot, placing the top oven shelf about 25cm below the heat elements.

Add 2 tablespoons of the cake batter to the prepared tin and spread it evenly with a pastry brush. Place it under the grill for about 2–3 minutes, until it starts to brown. Repeat this step until all the batter is used up.

Run a thin knife around the cake to loosen it, then turn it onto a wire rack and leave to cool upside down; this is how the cake should be served.

Once cool, brush the cake thinly with apricot jam and coat with the chocolate.

If stored in an airtight container, this cake will improve over the first couple of days, and will keep for a week.

MAKES 1 X 450G CAKE

5 eggs, separated
1 pinch salt
145g caster sugar (divided)
145g unsalted butter, plus extra for greasing
½ teaspoon vanilla bean paste
50g cornflour
90g plain flour
7g baking powder
100g apricot jam, warmed to help it spread
1 quantity Dipping Chocolate (see page 193)

When I was little we had some fruit trees (cherries, apples, pears, plums) in the garden, and we had our own raspberries, strawberries and gooseberries. We also went foraging for blackberries and blueberries. As a result, the use of fruit in my family was very seasonal. At Christmas, it was time to open some jars of preserved cherries or pears. But the fruit that took over towards Christmas was the orange. Suddenly we were using candied orange peel and orange oil in baking, and the gift bags of biscuits we prepared often contained oranges as well. From that memory comes my idea for this yule log: a rich chocolate sponge with a fragrant and light orange filling.

Jürgens Orange Bûche de Noël
Jürgen's Orange Yule Log

This recipe involves several cooling phases, so make sure to allow enough time to make this cake. Preheat the oven to 200°C fan/gas mark 7. Line a 40 x 30cm swiss roll tin with baking paper.

Place the ground almonds, icing sugar and honey in a food processor or blender and whizz together. Once they start to form a paste, add one of the egg whites. Transfer to a big bowl and set aside.

Whisk the egg yolks and 60g of the caster sugar in a bowl until fluffy and pale. Add the vanilla bean paste, then gradually fold in the egg yolk mixture.

Place the remaining 3 egg whites in a clean bowl and whisk to soft peaks. Keep whisking while adding the remaining 30g of caster sugar bit by bit. Continue until the egg whites are smooth and shiny, then fold them into the yolk mixture. Finally, sift in the flour and cocoa powder and fold together.

Spread the batter evenly in the prepared tin and bake for about 8 minutes. The sponge should feel soft and elastic. Leave to cool in the tin for a few minutes, then cover with a sheet of baking paper and turn it onto a wire rack. Don't remove the bottom baking paper yet, as it will help with rolling up the sponge. Set aside to cool completely.

SERVES 12–16

30g ground almonds
30g icing sugar
30g honey
4 eggs, separated
90g caster sugar
½ teaspoon vanilla bean paste
40g plain flour
30g cocoa powder

For the filling
2–4 oranges, preferably unwaxed, to give 260g of orange segments
110g caster sugar
160ml orange juice
25g cornflour
50ml orange liqueur, such as Cointreau
600ml double cream

For the syrup
50g caster sugar
50ml water
100ml orange liqueur

For the ganache
360g dark chocolate (at least 55 per cent cocoa solids)
200g double cream
20g honey
30g unsalted butter, at room temperature

To make the filling, start by removing the zest from one of the oranges and setting it aside. Now cut off both ends of the oranges; this is best done with a serrated knife on a chopping board. Stand each orange on end and cut downwards to remove the peel and membrane. Now cut between the membrane walls to release the naked segments. Collect the segments and juice – you'll need 260g in total. Cut each segment into 3 pieces and place them and their juice in a small saucepan along with the sugar and reserved orange zest. Add 100ml of the additional orange juice and bring to a simmer.

Meanwhile, in a small bowl, mix the cornflour with the remaining 60ml of orange juice.

When the segments are simmering, whisk in the cornflour mixture. Boil for 1 minute to gelatinise the starch, then take off the heat and stir in the liqueur. Transfer to a bowl, cover with clingfilm and set aside to cool completely.

To make the syrup. place the sugar and water in a small saucepan and bring to the boil. Pour the hot syrup into a heatproof bowl and set aside to cool. Once cool, add the orange liqueur, then set aside. Whip the double cream for the filling, taking care not to curdle it by overwhipping. It should be soft but stable. Fold it into the bowl of orange segments.

Carefully peel the baking paper from the sponge, then place the sponge back on top of the baking paper. Using a pastry brush, soak the sponge with the orange syrup.

With a short side of the sponge nearest you, spread it with the cream and orange filling, leaving a clear 2cm border along both short sides. The filling should be even and not too thick.

Starting at the side nearest you, roll up the sponge, using the baking paper underneath it to help you. Make a tight roll, but don't squeeze out the filling. Wrap it in the baking paper you have just used and place it in the fridge or freezer for at least 20 minutes.

In the meantime, make the ganache. Break the chocolate into small pieces and place in a heatproof bowl. Place the cream and honey in a small saucepan and bring to a simmer. Take off the heat for 1 minute, then pour the mixture into the chocolate and wait again for 1 minute. Now stir it well until all the chocolate has melted and been incorporated into the cream. Stir in the butter.

When ready, cover the roll with the ganache. Once it has almost set, use a fork or comb to create a tree bark pattern. Trim the ends.

If stored in an airtight container in the fridge, this cake will keep for up to 4 days. It is best eaten at room temperature.

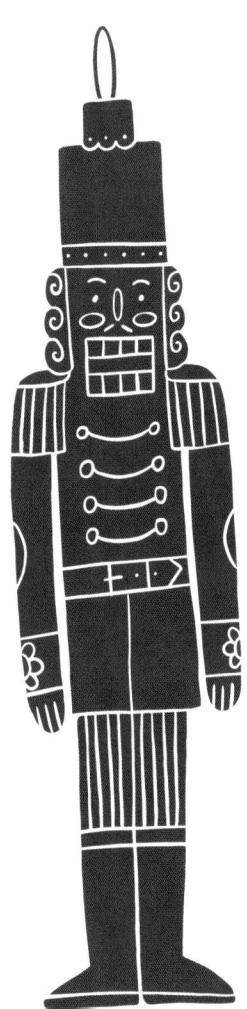

There is no equivalent word in German for 'pie', although there are traditional German bakes that have all the features of a pie. Very popular is this *Gedeckter Apfelkuchen*, which essentially means an apple tart with a lid. And a tart with a lid is, of course, a pie. The filling of this apple pie has taken inspiration from mulled wine.

Weihnachts-Apfelkuchen
Christmas Apple Pie

Put the apples into a saucepan along with the raisins, spices, muscovado sugar, lemon zest and half the wine. Bring to the boil, then cover and simmer for about 5 minutes, stirring occasionally to prevent burning.

When the apples have simmered, mix the remaining wine with the cornflour in a small bowl and stir it in. Simmer for another minute, then add the mixed peel. Set aside to cool.

Put all the pastry ingredients into a big bowl, mix to combine, then use your hands or a mixer fitted with a paddle attachment to form a smooth dough. Cover with clingfilm and set aside to rest for at least 30 minutes.

Preheat the oven to 200°C fan/gas mark 7. Line the base of a 23cm springform cake tin with baking paper and butter the sides.

Break off two-thirds of the dough and roll it out on a floured surface until about 3mm thick and 28cm wide. Use it to line the prepared tin. Trim off the excess.

Line the pastry case with crumpled baking paper and fill with baking beans. Blind bake for 15–20 minutes, until the rim is golden brown. Remove the beans and paper, then evenly spread in the filling.

Roll out the remaining dough on a floured work surface until you have a circle 23cm wide. Place it on top of the filling, and press around the edge to seal. Trim off the excess. Return it to the oven for another 15–20 minutes, until the lid is golden brown. Set aside to cool completely in the tin. Once cold, transfer it to a plate and dust with icing sugar, or glaze with lemon icing (made as on page 19) and decorate as desired.

SERVES 12

1.8kg tart, sharp-flavoured apples, such as Granny Smith, peeled, cored and chopped
50g raisins
2 teaspoons ground cinnamon
½ teaspoon ground cloves
¼ teaspoon ground mace or nutmeg
½ teaspoon ground allspice
50g muscovado sugar
zest of 1 lemon
80ml red wine
1 teaspoon cornflour
50g mixed peel
icing sugar, for dusting

For the pastry
350g plain flour, plus extra for dusting
1 teaspoon baking powder
125g caster sugar
20g vanilla sugar (for homemade, see page 194), or 1 teaspoon vanilla bean paste
175g cold unsalted butter, cubed, plus extra for greasing
1 pinch salt

For the lemon icing (optional)
150g icing sugar
lemon juice, as needed
food colouring (optional)

Town Band

Music has always played a big role in our family. My mother's father, my grandpa Erwin, joined the town band in Kappel in the early 1930s, first playing the cornet and later the euphonium. He also played percussion in some impromptu local dance bands, which did the rounds of some remote farms in the area that also doubled as dance venues.

Kappel was a tight-knit community, where everybody knew each other. When I look at the first photo of the town band that my grandpa appears in, taken at a wedding in 1936, I recognise the faces of many of the band members – musicians tended to join the band for a long time. My father played until he was 86!

It was on my father's trombone that I managed my first notes at the age of 12. My father then got me a beginner's trombone and taught me and my brother the fundamentals of brass playing. I soon became a member of the band, but my brother, although he proved a quick learner on my grandpa's euphonium, was more interested in pursuing athletics.

Band rehearsals were every Friday evening, and I was always impressed by my grandpa's preparations. About two hours before rehearsal time, the instrument was taken out, checked and possibly polished. He then shaved and put on a good shirt and a grey suit – he dressed for a special occasion. By the time I joined the band, the dress code was luckily more relaxed.

The band played at all kinds of events during the year, from church processions to beer festivals, but the highlight of the year was, of course, the Christmas concert. The male choir, also composed of members of the village, joined us. This concert involved by far the most preparation. Sometimes there was a weekend band camp somewhere in the middle of the woods, where we practised for two days solid.

On the day itself we spent the morning setting up long benches and trestle tables in the sports hall of the local school. Then the food and beverages would arrive – vats of beer, buckets of potato salad and steaming pots of sausages.

The concerts got better and better over time, with audiences of more than 500 people gathering from Kappel and all the surrounding villages as our reputation grew!

Members of the town band on their traditional walk through Kappel on New Year's Eve, c.1960. My grandpa Erwin is playing the euphonium, and my uncle Gerhard the clarinet.

Me posing in front of an amazing snowman my grandpa Erwin built in our backyard.

In my family there was never a Christmas without Linzer Torte. Named after the city of Linz in Austria, where it originated, this cake develops its flavour over time, and it also becomes less crumbly. My mother usually made several around mid-November and stored them until Christmas. My version uses Gingerbread Spice (see page 195) to give the cake an extra Christmassy feel.

Weihnachts-Linzertorte
Christmas Linzer Torte

Sift the flour, cocoa powder, almonds, sugar and spice into a big bowl. Add the butter and rub it into the flour mixture. Knead in the egg and liqueur until a dough forms, then knead until it holds together. If you have time, cover the dough with clingfilm and leave to rest in the fridge for 1 hour.

Preheat the oven to 175°C fan/gas mark 6. Grease a 23–25cm springform cake tin with some butter, then line with baking paper.

Set aside 200g of the dough. Place the remainder on a floured work surface and roll into a circle about 1cm thick and 2cm wider than your tin. Use this to line the prepared tin. There should be a rim all around, about 2cm high, so cut away any excess and use the offcuts to fill in any gaps (use some of the reserved dough if need be).

Prick the bottom of the pastry case with a fork. Decorate the rim if you wish – a traditional way is to squeeze a small section of the rim between the backs of two forks, then move to the next bit of the rim and do this all the way round.

Spread the bottom of the pastry case with a thin layer of jam. (The most important part of Linzer Torte is the pastry – it should not be overwhelmed by the sweetness of the jam.)

Roll out the reserved pastry until about 3mm thick and cut out strips for classic lattice work, or whatever decorative shapes you fancy. Place your decorations carefully on the jam, then brush them and the pastry rim with a thin layer of egg yolk. Bake for 30–40 minutes.

Let the Linzer Torte cool for at least 10 minutes before removing it from the tin. It will be quite fragile while hot. This tastes great on the day it is baked, but develops much greater aroma and flavour if stored for a week or longer in an airtight container. Dust with icing sugar before serving.

SERVES 12

240g plain flour, plus extra for dusting
30g cocoa powder
200g ground almonds
175g caster sugar
2 teaspoons Gingerbread Spice
  (see page 195)
200g cold unsalted butter, cubed,
  plus extra for greasing
1 egg
1 tablespoon almond liqueur (optional)
200g raspberry jam
1 egg yolk, beaten, for glazing
icing sugar, for dusting

Through my wife and her family, I was introduced to Jewish festivals and the specific foods connected with them. Honey is particularly associated with Rosh Hashanah (New Year), symbolizing the hope that the year to come will be sweet. When I first had Lekach, I immediately recognized its similarity to the honey cake we traditionally had in my family at Christmas, so it was like meeting an old friend. The colour and wonderful aroma of the cake comes from the rye flour and a long bake at low temperature.

Honigkuchen
Honey Cake or Lekach

MAKES 2 X 500G LOAF CAKES

90g brown sugar
2 teaspoons Gingerbread Spice (see page 195)
½ teaspoon baking ammonia (see page 59) or bicarbonate of soda
¼ teaspoon salt
1 egg
50ml vegetable oil
450g honey
125ml water
300g wholemeal rye flour
100g plain flour

Preheat the oven to 130°C fan/gas mark 2. Line two 500g loaf tins with baking paper.

Place all ingredients, except the flours, in a large bowl and beat together with an electric mixer at low speed. Once well combined, continue mixing while adding the flours bit by bit. Beat for another 5 minutes, until smooth.

Pour the batter into the prepared tins and bake for 2–2½ hours. Turn the cakes onto a wire rack and set aside to cool.

If stored in an airtight container, the cakes will keep for about 2 weeks.

Baking mini cakes in jam jars has been a bit of a fashion in Germany recently, and for several good reasons. This kind of cake is very easy to make, keeps unopened for three weeks, and makes an excellent gift. While the cake matures, the aroma of the fruit slowly penetrates the whole sponge, and because it is sealed, it won't dry out.

Früchtekuchen mit Zimt im Glas
Cinnamon Fruit Cake in a Jar

Make sure all the ingredients are at room temperature.

Preheat the oven to 170°C fan/gas mark 5. Grease 5 x 340ml jam jars. Put the lids in boiling water and set aside.

Sift the flour, baking powder and spices into a bowl and set aside.

Using an electric mixer, cream the butter and sugar together. When light and fluffy, beat in the eggs one at a time. Now stir in the flour mixture a bit at a time, then add the milk.

Divide the batter equally between the jam jars, making sure they are no more than half full.

Place a piece of fruit in the middle of each jar and push it down, then place a second piece of fruit in the middle and push it down lightly. The top half of this piece will still be visible on the surface.

Place the jars on a baking sheet. Bake, uncovered, for 25–30 minutes, until a skewer inserted into the cake comes out clean. When done, transfer the jars to a wire rack and put the sterilized lids on.

Serve the cakes with whipped cream or vanilla ice cream. They are delicious straight right away, but will develop their flavour over time. Provided the jars are unopened, the cakes will keep for 3 weeks.

MAKES 5 X 340ML JAM JARS

200g plain flour
16g baking powder
1 tablespoon ground cinnamon
¼ teaspoon ground cloves
125g unsalted butter or margarine, plus extra for greasing
120g brown sugar
3 eggs
1 tablespoon full-fat or semi-skimmed milk
10 cherry-sized pieces of fruit, such as pieces of apple, pear or plum

Bread – Sweet and Savoury

Joghurt Stollen
Yogurt Stollen 103

Buchteln
Sweet Filled Buns 104

Weihnachts-Scones
Christmas Scones 107

Weckmänner
Dough Men 108

Knuspriges Schwarzwälder Brot
Crusty Black Forest Loaf 113

Sourdough Starter 114

Roggenbrot
Rye Bread 118

Bread is one of the most fundamental foods in Germany, as is highlighted by the hundreds of different types sold in bakeries throughout the country. Bread is meant to have a strong flavour of its own and be just as delicious as the things you put on top of it.

Bread featured heavily in my childhood meals: we had a savoury breakfast with bread; lunch was a cooked meal, sometimes accompanied by bread; and supper was again bread with slices of sausage or cheese. These days, my parents usually have several very different loaves on offer.

In this chapter you'll find a couple of recipes that use a rye sourdough starter and make typically German breads with distinctive flavours to have at breakfast or supper. They vary in rye content and therefore have a different mouthfeel and flavour.

And of course, there are also breads for special holidays. Often sweet and enriched with butter, these include the dough men (see page 108) beloved by all children and many varieties of stollen. These stunning celebration breads are always welcome as gifts and easier to make than you might think.

The origins of stollen go back to the medieval tradition of fasting before Christmas, when bread was not allowed to contain butter or sugar. At some point the nobility of Saxony got permission from the Pope to use butter on condition that the stollen was taxed and the money used to build a cathedral. A hard, tough bread thus evolved into a rich and expensive sweet loaf. Some varieties of stollen – such as the protected 'Dresdner Stollen' – are quite involved to make and need a long time to mature, but this version can be eaten right away.

Joghurt Stollen
Yogurt Stollen

Soak the raisins and currants in the rum overnight.

Make sure your butter, milk, yogurt and eggs are all at room temperature before you start. Preheat the oven to 170°C fan/gas mark 5. Line a baking sheet with baking paper.

Place the flours in a big bowl along with the baking powder, caster sugar, almonds, salt and spices. Mix well with a whisk.

Combine the milk, yogurt, eggs and lemon zest in a separate bowl and whisk to combine. Add this mixture, along with the cubed butter, to the dry ingredients and mix with a big spoon or electric mixer until well combined.

Drain the dried fruit, add it to the dough with the mixed peel and knead it in until the dough becomes smooth and elastic. Set aside to rest for about 10 minutes.

Turn the dough onto a well-floured work surface and shape it into a flat rectangle about 25 x 18 cm. Fold the dough in half lengthways. Transfer the stollen to the prepared sheet and bake for about 70 minutes, until the top is dark golden brown. Set aside to cool on a wire rack. If making two small stollen, simply cut the folded dough in half and bake side by side on the prepared sheet for about 1 hour. Keep an eye on the colour towards the end of the baking time.

Melt the extra 150g butter and brush it all over the stollen. Let the butter set, then dust liberally with icing sugar. If stored in an airtight container or wrapped in foil, the stollen will improve over the first week, and will keep for 2 weeks.

MAKES AN 18 X 25CM STOLLEN
OR 2 HALF THAT SIZE

120g raisins
120g currants
150ml rum
300g strong white flour
200g plain flour, plus extra for dusting
16g baking powder
150g caster sugar
120g ground almonds
1 pinch salt
¼ teaspoon ground nutmeg
¼ teaspoon ground cloves
½ teaspoon ground cardamom
100ml full-fat milks, at room temperature
150ml full-fat Greek yogurts, at room temperature
2 eggs, at room temperature
zest of 1 lemon
120g unsalted butter, at room temperature, cubed, plus 150g for brushing
120g mixed peel
icing sugar, for dusting

Like many people, my mother had a fear of making yeasted doughs, having heard about the complications of using fresh yeast. But once fast-action dried yeast became available, she discovered that the process can be straightforward, so she started making these filled buns. They freeze very well and my mother now always has a bag of them in the freezer, ready to serve to unexpected guests.

Buchteln
Sweet Filled Buns

MAKES 16

250g strong white flour
250g plain flour, plus extra for dusting
30g caster sugar
1 x 7g sachet fast-action dried yeast
6g salt
1 egg
280ml milk, lukewarm
70g unsalted butter, melted, plus extra for greasing and brushing
1 teaspoon vanilla bean paste
icing sugar, for dusting

Suggested fillings
pitted prunes
soft dried apricots
Powidl (Austrian plum jam) or apricot jam

Place the flours in a large bowl along with the caster sugar, yeast, salt, egg, milk and melted butter. Mix until well combined, then knead for about 10 minutes, until a smooth dough forms. Cover with clingfilm and set aside to rest in a warm place for about 1½ hours. The dough should be well risen and feel fluffy.

Transfer the dough to a floured work surface and divide it into 60g pieces. Roll them into balls and set aside to rest for 10 minutes.

Grease a brownie tin or baking tray with some extra butter.

Flatten a dough ball and place 1 prune or apricot, or 1 teaspoon jam, in the middle of it. Carefully pull the edges of the dough over the filling and seal well. Turn upside down and place in the prepared tin or tray. Repeat with the remaining dough balls. The buns should just about touch each other. Cover and set aside to rise for 45 minutes.

Preheat the oven to 170°C fan/gas mark 5.

Once the buns have risen, brush them with some extra melted butter and bake for 25 minutes, until the tops are golden brown. Set aside to cool a bit before removing from the tin and dusting lightly with icing sugar. (If planning to freeze the buns, omit the icing sugar; it can be added after reheating them at 150°C fan/gas mark 3 for 10 minutes.)

These are very nice eaten slightly warm, served as a share-and tear bake, or with whipped cream or ice cream. If stored in an airtight container, they will keep for 3 days.

Scones are a very English thing, but in recent years have become popular in Germany too. Quick and easy to make, they offer infinite variations, sweet and savoury. Here I have incorporated my Gingerbread Spice to give a Germanic Christmassy twist.

Weihnachts-Scones
Christmas Scones

Preheat the oven to 180°C fan/gas mark 6. Line a baking sheet with baking paper.

Put the flour, sugar, baking powder, salt and spice into a bowl. Add the butter and rub it in using your fingers. Add the milk and cream and mix quickly by hand or with a wooden spoon until a dough forms. Now work in the chopped apricots and mixed peel.

Turn the dough onto a floured surface, then pat and stretch it out until about 3cm thick. Using a 5cm round cutter, stamp out 8 circles. Place them on the prepared tray, spacing them well apart. Brush just the top of them with beaten egg.

Bake for about 18 minutes. Owing to the spice content, it is tricky to judge the bake by colour – the egg glaze should be golden-brown. Set aside to cool, then serve with butter, cream and/or jam. If stored in an airtight container, these scones will keep well for 3–4 days without needing to be reheated.

MAKES ABOUT 8

200g plain flour, plus extra for dusting
30g caster sugar
7g baking powder
1 pinch salt
2 teaspoons Gingerbread Spice (see page 195)
50g cold unsalted butter, cubed
60ml full-fat milk
60ml double cream
60g dried apricots, chopped
40g mixed peel
1 egg, beaten, for brushing

These sweet breads shaped like little men are traditional in many parts of the German-speaking world, where they are known under a variety of names – Weckmann, Nikolaus-Mann, Stutenkerl and Grittibänz, to name just a few. They are often made around St Martin's Day (11 November) or St Nicholas Day (6 December), and during the Advent period. In our village, all the children participating in the lantern procession on St Martin's Day were given one of these dough men. If you give them to your German or Swiss friends, you will certainly conjure up some childhood memories for them!

Weckmänner Dough Men

If the butter is too cold, add it to the milk and microwave or heat gently on the hob until the mixture is lukewarm.

Put all the dry ingredients into a bowl and whisk to combine. Add the butter, milk and egg and mix well. Using your hands or an electric mixer fitted with a dough hook, knead the dough until it loses its stickiness and forms a smooth ball. Cover with clingfilm and set aside in a warm place for at least 1 hour, until the dough is well risen and puffy, with lots of air bubbles. Many baking recipes mention that the dough should 'double in size' – this is a somewhat unclear instruction, as the doubling could refer to the volume, or simply to the appearance of the dough, and those criteria are hard to measure.

Line 2 baking trays with baking paper and set them aside.

Divide the dough into 150g pieces. Set aside one piece, then roll the others into balls.

On a lightly floured surface (just enough to avoid sticking), use your hands to roll each ball into a plump log.

The next step is to create the head and body shape. With palms down, turn one hand at right angles to the other hand, with the little finger being near the work surface. Place the edge of your rotated hand near one end of a log and the other hand near the other end. Continue the rolling movement with both hands so that you end up with a skittle shape – a small head on a tapered body. Make 4 more bodies in the same way, then cover with a tea towel or plastic bag and leave to rest for a few minutes.

MAKES 5

60g unsalted butter, cubed, at room temperature
250ml full-fat milk, lukewarm
500g strong white flour, plus extra for dusting
60g caster sugar
2g salt, plus an extra pinch for the egg wash
1 x 7g sachet fast-action dried yeast
1 egg
raisins, as needed

For the egg wash
1 egg
1 pinch salt
2 tablespoons water
1 teaspoon milk

Flatten each body using a rolling pin or your hands, making sure the shoulders are the widest part, about 4cm wide, and that the lower end remains quite pointy. The length of the whole piece should by now be around 20cm.

Use a sharp knife or dough cutter to cut the arms, from the imagined hip up towards the shoulder, parallel to the spine. To form the legs, cut the lower body apart, from the pointed end to about halfway up the figure, where the arms start. Transfer to a prepared sheet and shape the arms and legs as you wish. To form the feet, cut halfway through the inside end of each dough leg, then turn the tips sideways.

To decorate, roll out the reserved dough ball thinly, about 1mm thick. Use a knife to cut about 10 strips of dough about 2mm wide and 10cm long, and 5 triangles with 4cm sides. Take a triangle and wrap it around the top half of the head to create a pointed hat. Use the strips to create a belt, and a scarf that you wrap around the neck and twist at the front. You can also use shorter strips to wrap around the legs, about 3 cm above the feet, this creates the effect of boots. Finally, push some raisins into the dough for eyes and buttons. Cover the figures and set aside to rest in a warm place for about 40 minutes.

To prepare the egg wash, break the egg into a bowl and mix in a pinch of salt, the water and the milk.

Preheat the oven to 170°C fan/gas mark 5.

Check the raisins on your figures – if they have risen to the top, push them back into the dough. Brush the egg wash onto your figures, then bake for about 15 minutes, until deep golden.

These are best eaten fresh, but can also be toasted for a great addition to the breakfast table. If stored in an airtight container, they will keep for 3 days.

The small amount of lard or coconut oil in this bread gives it a fairly closed crumb, while the use of both a rye starter and a wheat starter creates a rich, deep flavour.

Knuspriges Schwarzwälder Brot
Crusty Black Forest Loaf

Mix all the rye starter ingredients in a large container (about 3 times the volume of the fresh mixture), cover with a lid or clingfilm and leave to stand in a warm place for about 15 hours, until the mixture develops bubbles and smells yeasty. Alternatively, you can use a rye sourdough starter (see page 114).

Mix all the wheat starter ingredients in a large container (about 3 times the volume of the fresh mixture), cover with a lid or clingfilm and leave to stand in a warm place for about 15 hours, until the mixture develops bubbles and smells yeasty.

Once the starters are ready, add them to a large bowl with all the ingredients for the bread and mix thoroughly. Knead for about 10 minutes, until a smooth dough forms. It will be quite soft and remain a bit sticky. Cover with clingfilm and set aside for about 1 hour.

Grease a 500g loaf tin with some extra lard or coconut oil, then dust it with extra rye flour. With very wet hands, shape the dough into a log and place it in the prepared tin. Cover and set aside to rise for another hour.

Once the dough has risen, preheat the oven to 240°C fan/gas mark 9.

Uncover the dough and make a lengthways incision in it. Bake for 10 minutes, then reduce the temperature to 200°C fan/gas mark 7 and bake for another 10 minutes. Reduce the oven temperature again to 180°C fan/gas mark 6 and bake for another 25 minutes, until the crust is dark golden brown.

Turn the loaf out of the tin and set aside on a wire rack to cool completely. It will keep for 3–5 days, stored in an airtight container.

MAKES 1 X 600G LOAF

For the rye starter
45g wholemeal rye flour, plus extra for dusting
45ml water
¼ teaspoon fast-action dried yeast

For the wheat starter
140g wholemeal wheat flour
100ml water
¼ teaspoon fast-action dried yeast

For the bread
165g strong white flour
7g salt
½ teaspoon fast-action dried yeast
110ml water
5g lard or coconut oil, plus extra for greasing

There are many ways to set up a sourdough starter. I use the same process for wholegrain rye, wholegrain wheat and white wheat, and usually get good results. However, things can go wrong, and probably will, so don't hesitate to throw out a bad starter and begin again. This starter has 100 per cent hydration, meaning that it has equal amounts of flour and water by weight (All percentages refer to the total of flour used). These ingredients ferment by taking in yeast that is naturally present in the flour and in the air all around. A new starter takes 7–9 days to mature enough to use. The idea is to use just a portion of it, then 'feed' the remainder with fresh flour and water so that you never again need to create a starter from scratch.

Sourdough Starter

MAKES 80G

lukewarm water
flour of your choice

On the morning of Day 1, you start by combining 5g flour and and 5ml lukewarm water in a screwtop jar or plastic container that will hold triple the volume of the basic mixture. Cover loosely with a lid and set aside in a warm place (ideally 28°C for rye, and a little bit warmer than that for wheat). Over the first 5 days, you double the amount of water and flour every 12 hours and discard some of the mixture, as outlined opposite. Stir in every addition and cover loosely with a lid. After this 'doubling stage', the pattern changes.

TROUBLESHOOTING:

If a new starter continues to smell foul, or there is no gas production after the whole cycle has been gone through, discard it and try again. There might be an issue with the flour used, so perhaps try a different brand, preferably organic wholegrain flour, or grind up some rye grains yourself.

Day 1: Morning – Combine 5g flour + 5ml lukewarm water. Evening – Add 5g flour and 5g lukewarm water.

Day 2: Morning – Add 10g flour and 10ml lukewarm water. Evening – Add 20g flour and 20ml lukewarm water. You now have 80g of starter, and by the next morning you might see bubbles in it.

Day 3: Morning – Place 20g of the starter in a clean container, discarding the rest. Add 10g flour and 10ml lukewarm water. Evening – Add 20g flour and 20ml lukewarm water.

Day 4: Morning – Place 20g of the starter in a clean container, discarding the rest. Add 10g flour and 10ml lukewarm water. Evening – Add 20g flour and 20ml lukewarm water. At this stage you might see a lot of gas production and the starter might smell foul (unwanted leuconostoc bacteria). That's OK – the bacteria and yeasts are sorting out the good guys from the bad, so carry on. Most likely the good guys will win!

Day 5: Morning – Place 40g of the starter in a clean container, discarding the rest. Add 20g flour and 20ml lukewarm water. Evening – Add 40g flour and 40ml lukewarm water.

Day 6: Morning – Place 40g of the starter in a clean container, discarding the rest. Add 20g flour and 20ml lukewarm water. Evening – Add 40g flour and 40ml lukewarm water. At this point there should be less vigorous gas production, and a pleasant smell.

Day 7: Morning – Switch to the 'production cycle': all future refreshments (feeds) will use the following ratios. All percentages refer to the total of flour used. For rye, mix 50g flour (100%) and 50ml water (100%) with 2.5g starter (5%). For wheat, the flour and water amounts remain the same but use 10g starter (20%).

Day 8: One feed or refreshment as per Day 7.

Day 9: If the results of Day 7 and Day 8 are very similar in texture, smell and taste, you have a working starter! The smell should be pleasant and flowery, while the taste should be slightly acidic. All future refreshments follow Days 7–9. You are now ready to bake with your starter, or to store it (see page 116). Occasionally, a starter may appear inconsistent – not the same as Day 7 and Day 8. If this is the case, feed as on Day 8 for 2 more days. If the starter still does not perform, throw it away and start again.

Once the starter is established, keep it in a screwtop jar in the fridge. It won't need feeding for a few weeks, but take it out a day before you need it and revive it with a Day 7 feed. You need to keep only a small amount, so use the rest to flavour yeasted bread, replacing 10 per cent each of the flour and water in a recipe with the same weight of starter. Wheat starter is great for making pancakes.

Before baking, use lukewarm water to mix up your 'production starter' and create a surplus for next time. For example, if your recipe calls for 300g rye starter, make it using 160g flour + 160ml water + 8g starter = 328g production starter.

NOTES

- During the doubling stages (Days 1–6) the starter might develop more quickly than indicated, so if it does you can skip further doubling at that point and switch to the production cycle earlier.

- A rye starter can be used to 'seed' a wheat starter. This means using a small amount of rye starter to accelerate fermentation of a wheat starter, rather than beginning from scratch.

- If the starter has been in the fridge for a long time or has been a bit neglected, you can go through 2 feeding cycles (Days 7 and 8) before baking.

- Starters kept in the fridge can develop a mould-like skin. Just scratch that off and use the starter from underneath. It should still smell pleasant.

- Some starters can also develop a liquid on top (hooch); just stir it in.

- A 'hungry' starter smells of acetone (nail polish remover). So feed it!

Having a very high rye content, this loaf is dense and very aromatic. Rye contains enzymes that degrade gluten, so there is no kneading stage – the dough simply has to be mixed to get all the flour hydrated. Further mixing will make the crumb somewhat smoother, but is not essential. Instead of gluten as a binder, rye flour has complex sugars that hold the bread together, which means the dough is quite sticky. Use plenty of water on your hands and tools when working this dough.

Roggenbrot
Rye Bread

MAKES 1 X 500G LOAF

190g wholemeal rye flour, plus extra for dusting
70g strong white flour
160ml lukewarm water
7g salt
1 teaspoon fast-action dried yeast
200g rye Sourdough Starter (see page 114), or make the yeasted starter below
butter, for greasing

For the yeasted starter
100g wholemeal rye flour
100ml water
¼ teaspoon fast-action dried yeast

If making the yeasted starter, mix all the ingredients in a container that can hold about 3 times the volume of the fresh mix. Cover and set aside in a warm place for about 15 hours.

Once the yeasted or sourdough starter is ready, add it to a bowl containing the flours, water, salt and yeast and mix thoroughly. As mentioned above, kneading is not necessary, so simply cover the dough and let it stand in a warm place for about 1 hour. If you are using a sourdough starter, you can leave out the yeast, if you prefer – just increase this first rise to 2 hours instead.

Butter a 500g loaf tin, then dust it with some extra rye flour.

With very wet hands, shape the dough into a log and place it in the prepared tin. Cover and set aside to rise for another hour.

Preheat the oven to 240°C fan/gas mark 9.

Once the loaf has risen, dust it lightly with rye flour and make criss-cross cuts about 5mm deep on the surface. Bake for 10 minutes, then reduce the oven temperature to 200°C fan/gas mark 7 and bake for another 10 minutes. Finally, reduce the oven temperature once more to 180°C fan/gas mark 6 and bake for another 25 minutes, until the crust is chocolate-coloured.

Turn the loaf onto a wire rack and leave to cool completely. Ideally, it should rest overnight so that the crumb sets before being cut into.

St Martin's Day – the start of Christmas *Vorfreude* in Germany

My mother and my brother getting ready with their lanterns before the St Martin's Day procession

The German word *Vorfreude* means 'joyful anticipation', and for some people, the pleasure of looking forward to Christmas begins on 11 November. St Martin's Day is celebrated to commemorate Martin of Tours, a fourth-century Roman soldier who went on to become a bishop in Gaul. Legend relates a story of Martin's kindness when he was still a soldier: riding through a snowstorm, he encountered a beggar who had only rags to wear to protect him from the bitter cold. Martin took his sword, split his red wool cloak in half and gave one half to the beggar.

In many predominantly Catholic regions, St Martin's Day is an exciting day for children. In school and at kindergarten, they make paper lanterns of various designs, which they then carry through the village. When I was a child, these processions were quite big – two hundred people or more – as most of the local children took part, often accompanied by a parent or grandparent. The procession started at the church and wound its way past the houses to the school, guided by the priest and accompanied the church choir and the town brass band. They played the special St Martin's Day songs, and everybody sang along. My father was the trombonist in our town band, and every year, he would complain about having to play these songs in triple meter, like a slow waltz, and about how confusing it was to play like this while trying to walk in step with the other musicians.

Because all the lanterns were illuminated by candles back then, the lanterns were hung from from sticks, so that we could carry them in front of us without burning our fingers. Occasionally, if there was a strong wind blowing or a child couldn't keep their lantern steady, some of the paper lanterns would catch fire. Fortunately, nobody was harmed.

When the procession arrived at the school building, a little play recreating the scene with St Martin on horseback and the beggar was performed. Once the beggar had received his half of the cloak, the children were given their the *Weckmänner* pastries (see page 108). By this point, everyone would be getting a bit cold, and it was time to go home and have supper.

Festive Meals

Menu 1 125

Menu 2 133

Menu 3 141

Schinken im Brotteig
Gammon in a Bread Crust 153

Sauerkraut
Fermented Cabbage 155

Sauerkraut mit Äpfeln und Weißwein
Sauerkraut with apples and wine 157

Kartoffelbrei
Mashed Potato 158

Kartoffelsalat
Potato Salad 159

Spätzle
**Egg Noodles from
South-West Germany** 161

Käse-Spätzle
Spätzle with Cheese and Onions 162

Potato Croquettes 163

Bratäpfel
Baked Apples 165

Obst-Salat
Fruit Salad 166

Christmas is a busy time, and I remember my family always being on the go – there was the tree to decorate, festive meals to plan, visits to friends and family to organise. On top of all that, I also had altar boy duties at the local church.

Our big meal was always on Christmas Eve. The tree was put up in the morning, and the afternoon was free for cooking and experimenting in the kitchen. We didn't follow any particular traditions, but chose recipes that inspired us or made use of special ingredients we had at hand. After the main course and before dessert, there was the Bescherung, *when we exchanged gifts, because in Germany the* Christkind *(the Christ Child) brings presents on Christmas Eve! On the two following holidays, 25 and 26 December, the meals were quick. Often, we had potato salad with frankfurters or* Wienerle, *or mash with leftover meat.*

On the following pages are three menus for three-course meals as we had them on Christmas Eve at home. In addition, there are recipes for several quick meals, for those days when you really can't face another feast…

MENU 1

Grießklößchen-Suppe
Semolina Dumpling Soup

Hähnchen in Weißwein
Chicken in White Wine

*Schokoladenwaffeln
mit Kirschsahne*
Chocolate Waffles
with Kirsch Cream

Soups have always been a popular first course in Germany, and there is a huge variety of dumplings that are served in a clear broth. Apart from making a great starter, this soup can also be a standalone meal served with a slice of bread or crusty roll. My brother and I often enjoyed it as a quick lunch after school.

This soup can be prepared in advance and reheated, which makes it great as a part of a festive meal.

Grießklößchen-Suppe Semolina Dumpling Soup

SERVES 4

1.5 litres chicken stock
280ml full-fat milk
30g unsalted butter
1 pinch nutmeg
½ teaspoon salt
100g semolina
2 eggs
handful of chives, finely sliced, to serve

Place the chicken stock in a large saucepan and bring to a simmer.

Place the milk, butter, nutmeg and salt in a separate saucepan and bring to the boil.

Pour the semolina into the boiling milk while whisking, and continue whisking until the mixture forms a lump. Take off the heat and whisk in the eggs.

Using 2 teaspoons, or wet hands, immediately form the mixture into dumplings and lower them into the simmering stock. Once all the semolina mixture has been used, reduce the heat to its lowest setting so that the soup stops simmering but keeps warm. If you don't want to serve the soup straight away, let it cool and store in the fridge until needed. Reheat slowly without boiling.

Serve the dumpling soup sprinkled with chives.

Alsace is close to the area where I grew up, so its common food traditions inspired some of the festive meals we had at my childhood home in the Black Forest. As some lovely wines are produced in the region around Freiburg, it was obvious to use local wine in cooking, and it has a special place in this version of coq au vin.

Hähnchen in Weißwein
Chicken in White Wine

Heat a large flameproof casserole on the hob, then add one-third of the butter. When melted, fry the vegetables (apart from the mushrooms), until they start browning. Transfer to a plate and set aside.

Melt another one-third of the butter in the casserole and fry the mushrooms. Once they start releasing their liquid, add the garlic, stir briefly, then quickly remove the mushrooms with a slotted spoon and set them aside on another plate.

Melt the remaining butter in the casserole and fry the chicken pieces until the skin is well browned. Transfer to another plate and set aside.

Preheat the oven to 170°C fan/gas mark 5.

Pour half the wine into the casserole and bring to the boil while scraping up the crust from the bottom of the pan.

Add about half the vegetables and mushrooms, then stir in the salt and the herbs and add pepper to taste – about ½ teaspoon should work well. Add the chicken pieces and cover with the remaining vegetables and mushrooms. Add the remaining wine so that the vegetables are nearly covered. Wait until the wine boils, then cover with a lid and place in the oven for 2 hours.

When done, transfer the vegetables and chicken pieces to a serving platter. Be careful as the meat will slip off the bones easily. Keep warm.

To make a sauce, fast-boil the liquid left in the casserole until reduced by about half. Stir in the cream, then take off the heat and let it cool for a minute while stirring. Whisk in the egg yolk – the sauce should thicken slightly. For an even thicker sauce, you can purée some of the vegetables and stir them in too. Serve with egg noodles, such as Bandnudeln or Spätzle (see page 161), or with rice.

SERVES 4–6

100g unsalted butter
200g carrots, diced
200g onions, diced
200g celeriac, diced
250g leeks, sliced
100g celery, sliced
200g chestnut or portobello mushrooms, or a mixture, chopped if large, left whole if small
6 garlic cloves, crushed
1 x 2kg chicken, jointed into 6–8 pieces, or 6 chicken legs
750ml medium or dry white wine, ideally Riesling
2 teaspoons salt
1 fresh thyme sprig, chopped or 2 teaspoons dried thyme
1 bunch of fresh parsley, chopped, or 2 teaspoons dried parsley
pepper, to taste
50ml double cream
1 egg yolk

Waffles are always welcome, as is Black Forest gateau, so this dessert gives you a taste of both – a rich chocolate waffle served with Kirsch-flavoured whipped cream. I can see you going to the larder to look for some cherries now…

Schokoladenwaffeln mit Kirschsahne
Chocolate Waffles with Kirsch Cream

Place the chocolate in a heatproof bowl over a pan of simmering water (it must not touch the water). Stir from time to time while the chocolate melts. Alternatively, you can use the bain-marie method (see page 16).

Put the butter and half the caster sugar into a bowl and whisk until fluffy. Add the egg yolks and vanilla bean paste and whisk until they are fully incorporated.

Sift the flour, baking powder, cocoa powder and cloves into a clean bowl. Whisk small amounts of this into the egg mixture, alternating each addition with the milk and 50ml of the cream a bit at a time.

In a clean bowl, whisk the egg whites into soft peaks. Keep whisking while slowly adding the remaining 45g caster sugar, and continue until the mixture is smooth and shiny. Fold this into the batter, then fold in the melted chocolate.

Bake the waffles – the time will depend on your waffle maker. With this batter, you will get better results using a heart-shaped waffle maker than a Belgian waffle maker with a deeper grid.

For the topping, whip the remaining 250ml cream. When it starts to thicken, sift in the icing sugar bit by bit. Finally, add the Kirsch for a grown-up twist. Serve the cream with the waffles.

SERVES 4

70g chocolate (54 or 70 per cent cocoa solids), broken into small pieces
125g unsalted butter, cubed, at room temperature
90g caster sugar (divided)
3 eggs, separated
1 teaspoon vanilla bean paste
200g plain flour
½ teaspoon baking powder
40g cocoa powder
¼ teaspoon ground cloves
220ml full-fat milk, at room temperature
300ml double cream
30g icing sugar
10ml Kirsch

MENU 2

Räucherfisch Häppchen
Smoked Fish Canapés

Forelle Müllerin
Miller-style Trout

Weihnachts-Pavlova
Christmas Pavlova

Quick and easy to put together, the combination of dark rye bread, smoked fish and horseradish is a classic. The amounts of each ingredient you'll need depend on how many people you're feeding, but I suggest you allow 3–4 canapés per person.

Räucherfisch-Häppchen Smoked Fish Canapés

SERVES 4

rye bread (for homemade, see page 118)
butter, at room temperature
smoked salmon, or smoked trout
lemon juice
Horseradish Cream (see page 199)
small capers
cornichons, sliced

Cut the rye bread into thin slices about 4mm thick. Spread them with butter.

Using a small round cutter or the wide end of a large piping nozzle, stamp small circles out of the bread.

Use the same cutter to cut circles out of the smoked fish and place them on the bread circles. Sprinkle with lemon juice.

Using a spoon or a piping bag, place a dollop of creamy horseradish on the fish. Garnish with capers or cornichon slices.

Fish was always a popular dish in our family. When I was little, my grandfather was known to go down to the brook and catch us some trout with his bare hands! He taught me how to do it. My father relied on more conventional methods and took me fishing at some local ponds. When we were successful, we'd go home with trout, carp, bream, perch and other types of fish, which we often reserved for special occasions. A favourite way to serve trout, for example, was fried in butter and sprinkled with flaked almonds. In Germany, trout is often served with *Salzkartoffeln* (salted potatoes), but it also goes very well with steamed potatoes, especially baby ones.

Forelle Müllerin
Miller-style Trout

Cook the potatoes in boiling water with 2 teaspoons salt, simmering until tender. Drain, then return to the saucepan, cover with a lid and keep warm.

Pat the trout dry with kitchen paper. Season with salt and pepper and dust liberally with flour. Melt half the butter in a large heavy-based frying pan and cook the trout, turning them carefully twice. Depending on size, you may need 2 frying pans. They are ready when the bones separate easily from the flesh. Arrange the trout on a large serving platter. Place the cooked potatoes around them.

Melt the remaining butter in the same frying pan, add the flaked almonds and let them brown a little. Pour the melted butter over the trout, arranging some of the toasted almonds evenly over the top. Sprinkle chopped parsley over the trout and potatoes, then garnish with lemon slices and parsley sprigs. Serve with a green salad.

SERVES 4

For the potatoes
750g baby potatoes, unpeeled, or larger ones, peeled and cut into 6–8 chunks

For the fish
4 x 250g rainbow trout, cleaned and gutted
flour, for dusting
100g butter
100g flaked almonds
1 bunch curly parsley, finely chopped, but reserve a few sprigs for garnish
salt and freshly ground black pepper
lemon slices, to serve

Perhaps best known as a refreshing summer dessert, pavlovas usually feature plenty of fresh fruit on the chewy meringue base. Being for Christmas, this pavlova is a little different. To give it a warming quality it is sprinkled with cinnamon and cardamom, and generously topped with fruit that has been steeped in liqueur or rum for a long time.

Weihnachts-Pavlova
Christmas Pavlova

SERVES 4

For the meringue
6 large egg whites
300g caster sugar

For the caramelized walnuts
100g caster sugar
150g walnut halves

For the filling
200g white chocolate
600ml double cream
2 tablespoons icing sugar
1 teaspoon vanilla bean paste
3–4 oranges, segmented as described on page 85
prunes soaked in Armagnac, Rumtopf (see page 198) or similar
ground cinnamon
ground cardamon

Preheat the oven to 120°C fan/gas mark 1. Line a baking sheet with baking paper.

Place the egg whites in a large, scrupulously clean glass or metal bowl. Ensuring the beaters you intend to use have no trace of fat or dishwashing liquid, whisk the whites into soft peaks.

Continue whisking while adding the caster sugar a tablespoon at a time. Make sure each addition has dissolved completely before adding the next.

Spoon the meringue mixture onto the prepared sheet, forming a circle about 25cm wide. Use the spoon to create an attractive pattern around the side of it and form a central well to hold the fruit.

Bake for 75–80 minutes – the meringue should still be white. Switch off the heat and leave to cool completely in the oven with the door propped ajar with a wooden spoon or a rolled-up tea towel.

In the meantime, caramelize the walnuts. Put the caster sugar into a small heavy-bottomed saucepan and place over a medium heat. Stir the sugar until it starts to melt. If it melts and browns unevenly, tilt and rotate the saucepan a bit to gently mix the sugar, rather than stirring it. When the sugar starts to brown, add the walnuts to the pan and stir. Continue stirring and cooking for about 30 seconds, or until the sugar becomes golden brown. Don't let it burn!

Turn the caramelized nuts out onto a sheet of baking paper or a silicone mat immediately and use a knife or fork to separate. Be careful, boiled sugar is very hot! Set the caramelized nuts aside to cool.

When you are ready to assemble your pavlova, place the white chocolate in a heatproof bowl in the microwave and melt on High in short bursts of 10–20 seconds, stirring between each burst. Do not let it get hotter than 32°C. Alternatively, you can use the bain-marie method (see page 16).

Brush the central well of the cold meringue with the melted chocolate and let it set. This coating will prevent the meringue from becoming soggy if the pavlova stands for a while.

Whip the cream into soft peaks and gradually add the icing sugar and vanilla bean paste. Take care not to overwhip, as it will set a bit firmer while it stands. Spread the cream over the chocolate, then arrange the orange segments, alcoholic fruit and caramelized walnut halves on top. Sprinkle lightly with the cinnamon and cardamom, then transfer to a decorative platter and serve.

You can prepare the pavlova base (including the white chocolate layer) the day before, keeping it in an airtight container in a cool place.

MENU 3

Feldsalat
Lamb's Lettuce Salad

Weihnachts-Rindsrouladen
Christmas Beef Roulades

Weingelee mit Früchten
Wine Jelly with Fruit

Lamb's lettuce is a winter salad plant, most flavourful when harvested after the first frosts. The plants grow in little swirls that are used intact after the roots are trimmed off, which gives this salad lots of volume. This is the dish my family most looks forward to when visiting my parents in Germany for the Christmas holidays.

Feldsalat
Lamb's Lettuce Salad

Heat a dry frying pan and toast the walnut pieces until fragrant. Take care to stir often so they do not burn.

Using the flat side of a large knife, crush the garlic on a chopping board. Add the salt and continue to crush and scrape the garlic until a paste forms. Transfer it to a small bowl and stir in the oil, vinegar and a twist of black pepper until the dressing emulsifies.

Put the lettuce into a salad bowl and sprinkle with the toasted walnuts, carrot and onion. Add the dressing just before serving and toss well.

SERVES 4 AS A STARTER

2 tablespoons walnut pieces
1 garlic clove
¼ teaspoon salt
2 tablespoons sunflower oil or olive oil
1 teaspoon apple cider vinegar
200g lamb's lettuce, thoroughly washed
1 small carrot, grated
2 teaspoons finely chopped onion
freshly ground black pepper

Roulades (as beef olives are known in Germany) were a frequent Sunday dish in my family. They are fun to make, and my brother and I always enjoyed helping to prepare the stuffing and rolling up the little parcels. These are great to prepare in advance – they can sit uncooked in the fridge – and they have a fairly long cooking time, giving you more time with your guests. In a nod to my family's love of experimenting, I have used traditional English Christmas flavours in this festive version of the dish.

Weihnachts-Rindsrouladen
Christmas Beef Roulades

MAKES 5

- 5 thin slices beef steak (no more than 4mm thick), about 15–20 x 7cm, or any other cut of beef that is rich in connective tissue and suitable for long and slow cooking, such as a LMC or topside
- 5 teaspoons wholegrain mustard
- 100g butternut squash or carrots, cut into batons 5cm long
- 2 tablespoons vegetable oil
- 600g mixture of root vegetables (such as carrots, parsnips, swede, celeriac), chopped into 1cm cubes
- 1 potato, peeled and chopped into 1cm cubes
- 1 large onion, roughly chopped
- 4 garlic cloves, crushed
- 1 teaspoon salt
- ½ teaspoon freshly ground black pepper
- 500ml red wine
- 4 bay leaves
- 1 egg yolk

Start by combining all the filling ingredients in a bowl. Set aside.

Flatten the beef slices with a rolling pin or heavy-based pan. Spread 1 teaspoon of the mustard on each slice, followed by one-fifth of the filling, then add the squash or carrot batons. Roll up tightly and push 3 cocktail sticks through each roll to hold it together.

Preheat the oven to 170ºC fan/gas mark 5.

Meanwhile, heat the oil in a large flameproof casserole dish. When hot, sear the roulades briefly, taking care that they don't open. Remove from the casserole and set aside.

Add about half the cubed root vegetables to the dish and fry for several minutes until softened. Add the garlic and fry the mixture for another minute or so. Add the remaining cubed vegetables and continue frying and stirring for about 5 minutes. Add the salt, pepper and wine, stirring to scrape up and dissolve any crust on the bottom of the dish. Transfer the vegetable mixture to a plate.

Place the roulades in the dish, then cover with the cooked vegetable mixture. Pour in just enough water to cover the contents, then add the bay leaves. Cover with a lid and place in the oven for about 2 hours.

For the filling
- 100g butternut squash or carrots, cut into 5cm batons
- 125g mushrooms (such as portobello), finely chopped
- 60g pistachios or walnut pieces, finely chopped
- 100g vacuum-packed cooked chestnuts, finely chopped
- 100g dried cranberries
- 5 teaspoons wholegrain mustard
- ½ teaspoon salt
- ¼ teaspoon freshly ground black pepper
- 2 teaspoons herbes de Provence

When ready, transfer the roulades to a serving platter and keep warm. Strain the contents of the pan, returning the liquid to it but transferring the vegetables to a serving dish. Beat in the egg yolk to thicken the sauce. If you'd like it to be even thicker, purée some of the vegetables and stir them in.

These roulades can be served with Spätzle, mashed potato or other potato dishes, such as croquettes (see pages 161, 158 and 163). Don't forget to serve the reserved vegetables as a side dish.

A fruit jelly is a light and flavourful dessert after a rich meal, such as the roulades on page 144. Made with a good medium to dry white wine, it is quite refreshing. If you prefer, the gelatine can be swapped for agar-agar. In this case, please follow the packet instructions to determine the correct amount.

Weingelee mit Früchten
Wine Jelly with Fruit

Soak the gelatine leaves in a small bowl of cold water for 15 minutes. Meanwhile, place the sugar and wine in a saucepan, bring to the boil, stirring, then take off the heat. The sugar should be completely dissolved by now.

Squeeze the gelatine dry, then stir it into the hot wine to dissolve. Set aside to cool.

Layer the fruit into one big bowl or 6–8 ramekins. Once the wine jelly just starts to set, pour it over the fruit, making sure all the pieces are submerged. Cover with clingfilm and place in the fridge for several hours, until completely set.

To unmould the jelly, sit your bowl or ramekins in hot water for about 30 seconds, then invert onto a serving plate or dessert plates. Serve with whipped cream flavoured with cinnamon for a Christmassy touch.

SERVES 6–8

15 gelatine leaves
300g caster sugar
750ml white wine, such as Gewürztraminer or Riesling
500g seasonal or tropical fruit, such as peeled and chopped bananas, pears, apples, mangoes, grapes, orange segments, sliced or chopped into raspberry-sized pieces (do not include pineapple, papaya, figs or kiwi fruit, as these contain enzymes that will destroy the gelatine)

The Christmas Holidays

In early December, my mother, brother and I would start baking a selection of Christmas biscuits. These were all stored in a big tub with a lid that was kept in my parents' bedroom. This tub would gradually fill up over the course of the Advent season. Closer to Christmas Eve, my grandpa would take us into the forest, where we collected moss with which to decorate our nativity scenes while he was on his secret mission to find suitable candidates for our Christmas trees.

My grandparents' old farmhouse had been divided into four flats: my mother's parents lived upstairs, as did my aunt and her family, while my family lived in one of the two downstairs flats, with my great-grandmother and one of her daughters in the other. During the day on Christmas Eve, we would set up our nativity scene and put up the Christmas tree, getting everything ready for the *Christkind*, or Christ Child, to bring our gifts later that evening. My brother and I usually helped our grandfather and our great grandmother put up their nativity scenes and trees, too. My grandfather's nativity scene was always the most elaborate: it featured landscaped caves, all covered in moss, and took up a small dining table. It featured several sets of kings, and many angels, shepherds and sheep (quite a few of those sheep were missing a leg).

Getting everything ready involved retrieving all the decorations from the loft first. That loft was a magical place: there was old furniture up there, tables and lamps from the 1950s and all kinds of other things that were no longer considered fashionable. At the far end of the loft, below the only window, was a framed photograph of my great-grandfather Hermann Frey in his World War I uniform. The Christmas tree decorations were kept in an old tool cupboard that also contained all sorts of obscure and wonderful items. Among them was a small ancient bottle, well sealed, that contained mercury my grandfather had gathered from a huge broken barometer. The unexpected weight of this small bottle and its shiny liquid contents were fascinating to me.

For most of my youth, I was an altar boy at the local church, and Christmas was the busiest time of the year. All four Christmas services were packed: a Eucharist late on Christmas Eve (traditionally at midnight), then two on the morning of Christmas Day, followed by vespers that evening. The three Eucharists were spectacular, involving most of the available altar boys (around twelve of us per service), and every altar boy took part in at least two of those services. This put some constraints on our family life, but my parents didn't complain.

When I was a child, the shops in Germany were only open until 12.30pm on Saturdays, and they were closed on Sundays and public holidays. As we children got older, we were given some money at Christmas, and the school holidays between Christmas and New Year would have been a great opportunity to spend it, but the shopkeepers didn't think so. Visiting Freiburg in the days after Christmas was like going there on a Sunday – all the shops were doing their annual stocktake, and nothing was open.

My aunt Olga and my mother at Christmas, 1940. Many years later, my brother and I used some of those baubles and figurines to decorate the tree at my grandpa's.

Celebrating Christmas with my brother.

My family wasn't into making bread, so we children found it exciting to collect a pre-ordered batch of bread dough from the bakery. This dough, threatening to overflow its container, was clearly alive in a way I had no experience with. Back at home, my father cooked a *Schinken*, a cured and smoked pig's leg, until almost done. Then this huge piece of meat had to be wrapped in the bread dough, no easy task as the bone had sharp edges, and the live dough apparently had a mind of its own. But the result was always worth it. My favourite bits to eat were the pieces of bread crust richly soaked in meat juices.

Although using smoked pork is traditional in Germany, this recipe can be made with any smoked joint of meat.

Schinken im Brotteig
Gammon in a Bread Crust

Before cooking the joint, my butcher recommends soaking the gammon in 3 changes of cold water: first for 1 hour, then for 3 hours, and finally overnight.

The next day, place the drained gammon in a large pan, cover with fresh water and bring to the boil. Reduce the heat to a simmer, cover with a lid and cook for 1–2 hours. Drain the gammon and set aside to cool.

Combine the white flour, salt, yeast and oil in a mixing bowl.

If using the rye starter, add it now along with the water. Otherwise add the rye flour and water. Mix thoroughly, then knead for about 10 minutes, until a smooth, unsticky dough forms. Cover with clingfilm and rest in a warm place for 1–2 hours, until well risen.

Line a baking sheet with baking paper.

Turn the dough onto a floured work surface and roll out until about 1cm thick and large enough to encase the joint.

SERVES 6–8

800–1,200g gammon joint, smoked
3 tablespoons Dijon mustard
50g butter, melted

For the dough
400g strong white flour, plus extra for dusting
10g (2 teaspoons) salt
1 teaspoon dried fast-action yeast
10ml (2 teaspoons) olive oil
200g rye Sourdough Starter plus 220ml water (optional, see page 114) or 100g rye flour plus 320ml water

FESTIVE MEALS

Spread the mustard all over the cooled gammon, then place the joint upside down in the centre of the dough. Without stretching it, carefully wrap the dough around the gammon to cover it entirely, with no air pockets. Seal the dough along the join by squeezing the edges together and trim off any excess.

Place the wrapped gammon on the prepared baking sheet, seam side down, and prick several times with a fork so that steam can escape. The dough offcuts can be rolled out and used to make little decorations that can be stuck to the pastry case with water. Traditional shapes include braids or pig heads.

Cover the gammon with a clean tea towel and set aside to rest for 1 hour.

Preheat the oven to 210°C fan/gas mark 7½.

Brush the dough-covered gammon with the melted butter and bake for 10 minutes. Reduce the oven temperature to 200°C fan/gas mark 7 and bake for 20 minutes, then reduce the oven temperature again to 175°C fan/gas mark 6 and bake for 30 minutes more.

This festive-looking joint is best eaten hot in thin slices, with a green salad and Potato Salad or Sauerkraut (see pages 159 and opposite), but is also great cold. Wrap in foil and store in the fridge, where it will keep for up to 3 days.

An absolute staple in Germany, sauerkraut has been made at home for generations, or sold out of big tubs in grocery shops. But with cellars getting warmer due to central heating, people stopped using them for food storage and fermentation, and when I asked my grandma about making sauerkraut at home, she said, 'It's too complicated.'

With the big renaissance in fermenting food, it is now clear that making sauerkraut is not complicated at all, and here's how to make your own. The most important things are hygiene and plenty of salt. You will notice that this tastes different from ready-made sauerkraut, as you're unlikely to find the exact type of cabbage that is commonly used in Germany. However, white or pointed cabbage both work well.

Sauerkraut
Fermented Cabbage

Sterilize a 2-litre jar and its lid (see page 157).

Weigh a large bowl, then zero the scales, and weigh the prepared cabbage in it. Calculate 2 per cent of that figure, then add that amount of salt. Mix well, crushing it into the cabbage with your hands. Mix in the juniper berries, then set aside for about 1 hour, until brine starts to collect in the bowl.

Add the cabbage to the sterilized jar a handful at a time, using a blunt-ended rolling pin, or a special tool called a *Kraut-Stampfer*, to press down each addition.

Finally, add the juices from the bowl. The salt should have drawn enough liquid from the cabbage to ensure the contents of the jar are just about covered. Add a fermentation weight or other heavy object (a ramekin or a stone wrapped in clingfilm, for example) that will fit in the jar to keep the cabbage submerged.

Fasten the lid loosely, then label and date, and keep the jar out of sunlight. After a few days you should notice bubbles in the jar and that the cabbage has started to taste acidic. Continue fermenting until the flavour is to your liking, which may take up to 6 weeks, then store in the fridge and use as you wish.

MAKES ENOUGH TO FILL A 2-LITRE JAR

about 1.5kg white or pointed cabbage, finely sliced
salt – 2 per cent of the cabbage weight
15 juniper berries

Every region of Germany has its own way of cooking sauerkraut. Here is a good basic recipe, which my mother often uses.

Sauerkraut mit Äpfeln und Weißwein
Sauerkraut with apples and wine

Heat the butter or oil in a large saucepan, then fry the onion and lardons/sausage pieces until softened and slightly browned.

Add the sauerkraut, apple and bay leaves. Pour in enough wine or stock to just about cover the mixture. Bring to the boil, then cover and simmer for 20 minutes, stirring occasionally and topping up the liquid as needed.

This goes well with dishes such as Gammon in a Bread Crust (see page 153), or with sausages and mash.

SERVES 4

20g butter or oil
1 small onion, sliced
about 150g bacon lardons,
  or diced sausages
500g sauerkraut, drained
1 sharp-flavoured apple, such as
  Granny Smith, cored and diced
2 bay leaves
white wine or stock, as needed

HOW TO STERILIZE GLASS JARS

Wash both the jars and their metal lids on the hottest cycle in a dishwasher, or wash them by hand in hot soapy water, rinse well and place upside down on a baking sheet in a low oven for about 30 minutes.

Potatoes are amazingly versatile, and the mashed version of them can be made in a huge variety of ways. This is my mother's method and is hard to get wrong – unless, as I once did, you mash the potatoes in a blender. The result was an inedible gloop, because the blades of the blender damage the cells of the potatoes, releasing starch and turning the mixture into glue. Using a masher or potato ricer gives the best result.

Kartoffelbrei
Mashed Potato

SERVES 4

1.5 kg unpeeled potatoes, scrubbed but left whole

about 200g parsnips (optional), peeled and left whole

1 teaspoon salt

½ teaspoon coarsely ground black pepper

1 bunch of curly parsley, finely chopped

100g unsalted butter

125ml full-fat milk

Place the potatoes and parsnips in a large saucepan of cold water and bring to the boil. Reduce the heat and simmer until the potatoes are just tender. Don't overcook.

When ready, drain immediately. Leave the potatoes in the colander. Return the parsnips to the pan and mash until free of lumps. Transfer to a bowl.

Wearing rubber gloves, peel the potatoes while still piping hot. Return them to the empty pan and mash them with a masher or potato ricer.

Add the parsnip mash to the potato, along with the salt, pepper, 1 tablespoon of the parsley and 50g of the butter, and continue mashing until everything is well combined.

Place the milk in a small saucepan and bring to the boil. Meanwhile, reheat the pan of mash over a low–medium heat, taking care not to burn it.

Whisking the mash constantly, gradually add the boiling milk. Once incorporated, take the mash off the heat and transfer to a warm serving bowl.

Heat the remaining butter in a small frying pan and let it brown slightly. Pour this over the mash, then sprinkle with the remaining chopped parsley.

I've always loved this type of potato salad, which is made with a vinaigrette rather than mayonnaise. In my opinion, this dressing allows more of the potato flavour to come through. The salad also improves if left to stand for a few hours before serving, which makes it ideal for keeping in the fridge, ready to use in the quick meals required over the Christmas holiday period.

Kartoffelsalat
Potato Salad

Boil or steam the potatoes until they are soft but not fragile. Drain, then peel them (wearing rubber gloves), and set aside to cool completely.

Heat a small amount of oil in a frying pan and fry the lardons or sausage pieces until crisp and fragrant. Set aside on a plate lined with kitchen paper.

Once the potatoes are cool, slice them and place in a salad bowl. Add the chopped pepper and onion, plus the lardons or sausage (if using).

Place all the vinaigrette ingredients in a small bowl or screwtop jar and mix or shake until they emulsify. Pour this dressing over the potatoes and toss gently. Stir in the chopped parsley, and garnish with the parsley sprigs. Leave the salad to stand for at least a few hours before serving.

SERVES 4

750g salad potatoes
vegetable oil, for frying
2 tablespoons bacon lardons or chopped sausages (optional)
1 tablespoon finely chopped red pepper
1 tablespoon finely chopped white or red onion
handful of curly parsley, chopped, plus a few extra sprigs, to serve

For the vinaigrette
3 tablespoons extra virgin olive oil
1 tablespoon apple cider vinegar
½ teaspoon salt
¼ teaspoon freshly ground black pepper

My father has always been the Spätzle Master in my family. With the most meticulous attention to detail, he prepares the batter, adjusts its viscosity and scrapes thin strips of it into a big pan of boiling water. The result is adored by the whole younger generation in the Krauss family. There is no visit to my parents without having Spätzle. The skill has now been passed on to my son!

My father uses a *Spätzlebrett*, which looks like a cutting board with a handle. The short, straight end of the board tapers to a sharp edge, which helps to release the strips of batter and lets them fall into the water. It is made of wood that has been specially selected to stay straight, and must never be used as a chopping board, as that might warp it and render it unusable. If you don't have one, you can use a small cutting board with a handle instead.

Spätzle
Egg Noodles from South-West Germany

Place the eggs and extra yolk in a large bowl, add the salt and whisk until frothy. Using a wooden spoon or a mixer fitted with a dough hook, work in the flour, semolina, nutmeg and water bit by bit, until a smooth dough forms. It should still be very sticky and runny enough to slowly drip off the spoon or hook. When pulled, it should tear off in thin sheets, appearing to contain big bubbles. Cover and set aside to rest for at least 1 hour.

Once ready to cook, bring a large pan of salted water (at least 3 litres) to the boil. Place another large pan of cold water nearby. Set out a *Spätzlebrett* or small cutting board (ideally with a handle), plus a dough scraper, or a knife with a straight back, along with a wooden spoon and a slotted spoon or spider strainer. Finally, set out a platter for depositing the cooked noodles.

Dip your board and your scraping tool in the boiling water. Smear a spoonful of dough thinly onto the board, then use your scraper or the back of the knife to scrape thin strips of dough (no more than 2mm wide) into the boiling water. Repeat this with 2 or 3 more smears of dough. Cook for a further minute, then lift the Spätzle out of the boiling water with your slotted spoon and give them a quick dip in the cold water before placing them on the platter. Repeat until all the dough has been used up.

These Spätzle can be eaten right away as a side to dishes with gravy or sauce, such as goulash. Alternatively, they can be stored in the fridge for up to 3 days, then reheated in boiling water, or as we prefer them, fried in vegetable oil or butter until they crisp up slightly.

SERVES 4

3 eggs, plus 1 extra egg yolk
1 teaspoon salt
300g plain flour
50g fine semolina
1 pinch nutmeg
about 160ml water

Avid skiers will have had this hearty dish on trips to the Alpine region. It is very easy and quick to put together, as the Spätzle can be made in advance, or even be bought ready-made from delis. A mix of cheeses works very well, but do make sure that at least one of them is strongly flavoured.

Käse-Spätzle
Spätzle with Cheese and Onions

SERVES 2 AS A MAIN

500g Spätzle (see page 161)
200g cheese, such as Gruyère or Emmental, grated
oil for frying (optional)
300g onions, sliced into rings
butter, for frying
3 tablespoons finely chopped curly parsley
½ teaspoon salt, or to taste
freshly ground black pepper

There are 2 ways of preparing this recipe. The first is to layer the Spätzle and cheeses in an ovenproof dish and bake at 200ºC fan/gas mark 7 for about 15 minutes.

The second method is to fry the Spätzle in a little oil until they crisp up, then stir in the cheeses and continue frying until they have melted around the noodles.

Meanwhile, use a separate pan to fry the onion rings in some butter. Once they start to crisp up, add 2 tablespoons of the parsley, the salt and pepper and continue to fry for another 2 minutes.

Serve the Spätzle topped with the onions. As this dish is quite rich, it is nice to offer it with a small green salad (such as lamb's lettuce, see page 143) on the side.

My brother and I just loved croquettes. I remember the simple joy of tearing the crisp brown cocoons apart to reveal the soft, fragrant and steaming interior. If we had a choice, we'd always choose croquettes rather than French fries.

Potato Croquettes

Boil the potatoes until tender, then drain. Wearing rubber gloves, peel them immediately. Return them to the pan, then mash with a masher or potato ricer. Set aside to cool completely.

Once the potatoes are cold, mix in the egg yolk, along with the cornflour, 50g of the plain flour, the butter, salt, pepper and nutmeg.

Place the mash on a well-floured work surface and roll into a log about 2cm in diameter. Cut the log into croquettes 5cm long.

Set out 3 wide, shallow bowls. Lightly beat the egg white in one, place the remaining 100g flour in a second, and add the breadcrumbs to the third. Roll each croquette first in the flour, then in the egg white, and finally in the breadcrumbs, making sure they are well coated.

Pour a 7.5cm depth of vegetable oil into a large pan. Place over a high heat and bring it to 170°C, checking the temperature with a food thermometer. Alternatively, test it by dropping in a small cube of bread, which should brown in 20 seconds.

Once the oil is hot enough, deep-fry the croquettes for about 4 minutes, until crisp and golden on all sides. You may need to fry these in batches, so as not to overcrowd the pan, which will reduce the oil temperature and prevent the croquettes from crisping up.

SERVES 4

400g unpeeled potatoes, such as King Edwards, scrubbed but unpeeled
1 egg, separated
15g cornflour
150g plain flour (divided), plus extra for dusting
25g unsalted butter, at room temperature
¼ teaspoon salt
1 pinch freshly ground black pepper
1 pinch nutmeg
100g breadcrumbs
vegetable oil, for deep-frying

Here is a great dessert or teatime snack for a cold winter's day. My grandpa Erwin sometimes baked apples (without filling) on a plate on top of the wood-fired oven in his living room, and I remember eating them while watching *The Avengers* on his black-and-white TV set. Happy days...

Bratäpfel
Baked Apples

Preheat the oven to 200°C fan/gas mark 7. Line a baking sheet or shallow ovenproof dish with baking paper.

Core the apples, making sure they remain whole. Place them upright on the prepared sheet.

Put the raisins in a small bowl and mix in the walnuts, mixed peel, sugar, cinnamon and rum or orange juice. Carefully spoon this mixture into the apples, piling it on top too if you have enough. Bake for about 25 minutes.

Eat hot, with whipped cream or vanilla ice cream if you like.

SERVES 4

4 large, firm apples, such as Granny Smith or Gala
4 tablespoons raisins
2 tablespoons walnut pieces
1 tablespoon mixed peel
1 tablespoon muscovado sugar
1 teaspoon ground cinnamon
2 teaspoons rum or orange juice

While fruit salad can be made all year round, it is best made with seasonal fruit. However, that's not always possible, especially in winter, when many of us have to rely on imports. This version uses fruit that is generally available in the shops around Christmas, but feel free to make substitutions. The great thing about fruit salad is that it can be prepared in advance and matures in flavour if left to stand.

Obst-Salat
Fruit Salad

SERVES 8

2 apples, peeled, cored and chopped
2 pears, peeled, cored and chopped
2 bananas, peeled and chopped
1 regular orange, peeled and chopped
1 blood orange, peeled and chopped
juice of 1 lemon
¼ teaspoon ground cardamom
1 tablespoon brown sugar
2 tablespoons Kirsch

Combine all the fruit in a bowl, then add the lemon juice, cardamom, sugar and Kirsch. Mix well and set aside to stand for at least 1 hour before serving. Offer it with whipped cream or ice cream if you like.

This fruit salad will keep covered in the fridge for up to 2 days.

Christmas Market Food

Gebrannte Mandeln
Roast Almonds 173

Lebkuchen-Herzen
Gingerbread Hearts 175

Belgische Waffeln
Belgian Waffles 179

Magenbrot
Gingerbread Bites 182

Reibekuchen
Potato Cakes 185

Glühwein
Mulled Wine 186

Tee mit Rum
Tea with Rum 187

Kaffee Kirsch
Black Forest Coffee 188

German-style Christmas markets have become very popular internationally and they share many characteristics with the Christmas markets I remember from my childhood. Apart from being a treasure trove of artisanal products, perfect for stocking up on presents and decorations, there is always plenty of food and drink on offer.

As you drift along with the crowd through the twisting passages of a Christmas market, every stall offers a unique blend of colourful items, while the scents of the market are just as exciting and random as the sights – I remember the scent of incense, mulled wine, waffles, fried sausages, Gebrannte Mandeln (roast almonds), Black Forest ham and gingerbread.

What could be better after a couple of hours of shopping in the cold than a glass of mulled wine or spiced hot cider? There is always a non-alcoholic option, too. In case the mulled wine leaves you a bit lightheaded, you might want to find a Belgian Waffle, or some Reibekuchen (potato cakes). You could also buy some boiled sweets or a bag of Magenbrot to take home. And what could be a better gift for a loved one than a personalized gingerbread heart?

During the cold months of the year in Germany, sellers of roasted almonds pop up at every street corner and, of course, at Christmas markets as well. The almonds are prepared on the spot in copper colanders with cinnamon and caramel; the aroma they emit is just irresistible. It plays a huge part in creating a cosy Christmas market atmosphere.

Gebrannte Mandeln
Roast Almonds

Melted sugar gets very hot – well over 100°C – so be very careful and make sure you don't get distracted, as burns tend to be deep and painful.

Line a baking sheet with baking paper and set aside.

Place a steel or iron preserving pan or wok over a high heat. Add the sugars, cinnamon, cloves and water and bring to the boil, stirring the syrup constantly.

Add the almonds and keep stirring until the sugar crystallizes, then continue stirring until the nuts are done to your liking. Some people like them encrusted in little sugar lumps, while others prefer them to be more caramelized, with just the occasional lump of sugar. The timing depends on your equipment.

When the almonds are ready for you, turn them onto the prepared sheet and separate them with a spatula or spoon. They can be eaten slightly warm, or left to cool, then stored in an airtight container, where they will keep for several days.

MAKES 4 SMALL PORTIONS

100g caster sugar
15g vanilla sugar (for homemade, see page 194)
½ teaspoon ground cinnamon
⅛ teaspoon ground cloves
50ml water
150g whole almonds, with skin

Perhaps the best known of German biscuits outside Germany, Lebkuchen hearts are to be found at German funfairs, as well as at Christmas markets. Traditionally, they are decorated with royal icing symbols, greetings and quips appropriate to the time of year. This means many people like to keep them as souvenirs, but I prefer to eat them.

Lebkuchen-Herzen
Gingerbread Hearts

First make the starter, at least 2 days ahead of making the hearts: put the honey and molasses or black treacle into a saucepan and heat to 50°C while stirring constantly. Put the water and sugar into another saucepan and bring gently to the boil, stirring, then continue to boil without stirring until the mixture reaches 108°C. Let both liquids cool to about 30°C.

Once cool, mix the liquids together, then add both flours and mix again. Transfer to an airtight container and refrigerate for at least 2 days.

Before making the dough, allow the starter to come to room temperature. Line a baking sheet with baking paper and dust with extra flour.

Place the flour in a large bowl. If using baking ammonia, dissolve it in the milk and mix it into the flour along with the bicarbonate of soda. If using baking powder, mix it into the flour along with the bicarbonate of soda and the milk. Add the egg yolks, spice, salt and starter and mix until a smooth dough forms. Transfer the dough to the floured baking sheet, then flatten it and cover with clingfilm. Place in the fridge overnight.

Preheat the oven to 210°C fan/gas mark 8. Line 2 baking sheets with baking paper.

MAKES 40 SMALL HEARTS
OR 4 BIG HEARTS

For the starter
350g honey
50g molasses or black treacle
40ml water
80g caster sugar
300g rye flour
100g strong white flour

For the gingerbread hearts
2 teaspoons baking ammonia (see page 59) or baking powder
50ml full-fat milk
7g bicarbonate of soda
150g strong white flour, plus extra for dusting
2 egg yolks
2 tablespoons Gingerbread Spice (see page 195)
2g salt
2 egg whites, lightly whisked, for glazing

For the royal icing
2 egg whites
400g icing sugar, sifted, plus extra if needed
lemon juice, as needed
food colouring (optional)

Flouring a work surface as lightly as possible, roll out the dough until 6mm thick. Using heart-shaped cutters or templates of different sizes (they can be up to 25cm wide), cut out the Lebkuchen and transfer them to the prepared sheets. At this point, you can, if you like, pierce 2 holes in each heart (see photo opposite). Once baked, string or ribbon can be threaded through so they can be hung up as decorations or worn as a necklace. Brush the hearts lightly with some of the egg white.

Bake for 10–14 minutes, until dark brown. Immediately after removing the hearts from the oven, lightly brush them again with egg white. Set aside to cool.

To make the royal icing, beat the egg whites until frothy. Fold in the sifted icing sugar bit by bit. Add some lemon juice and whisk the icing until it is stiff and bright white. You want it to hold its shape when piped, so adjust the stiffness with additional lemon juice or icing sugar. Add food colouring to batches of the icing, as desired. Transfer to a piping bag fitted with a fine nozzle and pipe your chosen designs onto the hearts.

If stored in an airtight container, these Lebkuchen keep very well and should be left to improve for at least a week before eating. Note that they should be slightly soft and chewy, rather than hard and brittle.

TROUBLESHOOTING:

Note that if you don't have heart-shaped cutters, you can make your own cardboard templates and cut around them with a sharp knife.

These waffles are always very popular, not just at Christmas. To turn them into a festive treat, serve them with spiced apple sauce, cinnamon sugar or whipped cream flavoured with Kirsch. (Of course, you will need a waffle iron for this recipe – a Belgian waffle maker with deep pockets will work best.)

Belgische Waffeln
Belgian Waffles

Place the milk in a bowl and microwave on High for about 20 seconds, until lukewarm. Mix in the yeast, 1 teaspoon of the caster sugar and 1 teaspoon of the flour. Set aside for about 20 minutes, until it starts to froth.

Once the yeast mixture is ready, place the remaining flour in a large bowl and add the remaining caster sugar, the salt, vanilla bean paste, cream, egg and yeast mixture. Mix well, then knead by hand or with a mixer fitted with a dough hook, working in the butter bit by bit. Once the dough is smooth and elastic, cover with clingfilm and set aside in a warm place for 1½ –2 hours, by which time it should be well risen.

Sprinkle the pearl sugar over the dough and carefully work it in while also releasing the gas (a dough scraper is good for this). Cover the dough again and set aside to rest for another 10 minutes.

Divide the dough into pieces suitable for your waffle iron (about 80g each). Roll them into balls and set aside to rest for a few minutes. Cook them in your waffle iron until well caramelized. Eat warm.

These waffles can be stored in an airtight container for up to 3 days, then toasted to reheat them.

MAKES 8

70ml full-fat milk
1 x 7g sachet fast-action dried yeast
20g golden caster sugar
250g strong white flour
1 pinch salt
½ teaspoon vanilla bean paste
70ml double cream, at room temperature
1 egg
125g unsalted butter, at room temperature
90g pearl sugar or sugar nibs

CHRISTMAS MARKET FOOD

Christmas Markets

There have been Christmas markets in cities such as Munich, Frankfurt and Vienna, among others, since the fourteenth century, and they are still going strong there and in many other places today. The timing of Christmas markets also dates back to the Middle Ages: most of them start on the Saturday before the first Sunday of Advent (which is the fourth Sunday before Christmas) and end on 23 December or on the morning of Christmas Eve.

Christmas markets were originally held to help citizens buy the provisions they needed to get through the winter, but soon craftsmen were also allowed to sell toys and other gifts alongside those necessities. When I was little, the goods sold at the local Christmas market were not so very different from what you would have found there 200 years ago – there were stalls selling food, *Glühwein* and other adult beverages, sweets, gingerbread, toys and Christmas-related crafts, such as Christmas tree decorations and figurines for nativity sets.

In recent years, food and drink have become a much bigger part of Christmas markets, both in terms of quantity and diversity, and there are stalls selling imported products rather than just locally made things. But Christmas markets are still very atmospheric, especially if you visit them after dark, under the twinkling lights.

My mother, my brother, my grandma Ida and me on a family outing to Hofsgrund in the Black Forest, c. 1970

My grandma Ida would never come home from the Christmas market without a big bag of *Magenbrot* (literally 'stomach-bread'), a kind of gingerbread traditionally sold at Christmas markets and funfairs in cone-shaped paper bags. Unlike other types of gingerbread, it is best eaten within a couple of days of making, as after that, the glaze gets a bit sticky.

Magenbrot Gingerbread Bites

MAKES ABOUT 30 PIECES

300g plain flour, plus extra for dusting
150g wholemeal flour
140g brown sugar
1 teaspoon baking ammonia (see page 59) or baking powder
20g cocoa powder
1 tablespoon Gingerbread Spice (see page 195)
1 pinch salt
80ml milk
80ml water
140g honey

For the glaze
150g dark chocolate, 54–70 per cent cocoa solids, broken into pieces
30g unsalted butter
150ml water
375g icing sugar
1½ teaspoons Gingerbread Spice (see page 195)

Put the flours in a bowl with the sugar, baking ammonia or baking powder, cocoa powder, spice and salt and mix well. Add the milk, water and honey and mix until you have a smooth batter. If using baking ammonia, set the dough aside to rest for several hours. Otherwise, proceed straight to the next step.

Preheat the oven to 160ºC fan/gas mark 4. Line a baking sheet with baking paper.

Lightly flour a work surface. Divide the dough into 3 equal pieces and roll them into logs about 3cm in diameter. Place them on the prepared sheet and bake for 15–20 minutes. Transfer to a wire rack and leave to cool completely.

Cut the cooled logs into diagonal slices 2cm thick. Crumble the irregular end pieces into a small bowl and set aside.

To make the glaze, place the chocolate, butter and water in a large heatproof bowl and melt in short bursts on High in the microwave. Stir to combine. Sift in the icing sugar and spice and stir until smooth. Finally, stir in the reserved crumbs.

Dip the Magenbrot slices in the glaze, making sure they are evenly coated, and leave to dry on a wire rack for at least 2 hours.

If stored in an airtight container, these gingerbread bites will keep for 2 days.

Also known as *Kartoffelpuffer*, these potato patties are another crossover between German and Jewish cuisine, which knows them as latkes. Latkes are especially associated with the Jewish festival of Hanukkah, which celebrates the miracle of the temple lamps that burned for eight days despite having only enough oil for one day. Food made or cooked with oil is eaten in memory of that miracle, which is celebrated around Christmastime. However, *Reibekuchen* are eaten all year round, and are especially welcome as a snack on a cold winter's afternoon – and are therefore a classic Christmas market treat.

Reibekuchen
Potato Cakes

Place the potatoes and onion in a large bowl. Add the egg, salt, pepper and oats and mix well.

Pour enough oil into a large frying pan to cover the base well and place over a high heat. When hot, add mounds of the potato mixture – about 2 tablespoons per mound – and spread each out thinly with the back of a spoon. Fry on both sides until golden brown.

Serve with apple sauce.

SERVES 4

750g potatoes, finely grated
100g onion, finely grated
1 egg
½ teaspoon salt
freshly ground black pepper
1 tablespoon porridge oats
vegetable oil, for frying
apple sauce, to serve

Making your own mulled wine is very easy, and it fills the house with delicious Christmas aromas. You might be tempted to think that the spices will mask the flavour of inferior wine, but believe me – the better the wine used, the better the result.

To make a non-alcoholic version, use a mixture of grape juice and apple juice instead of wine.

Glühwein
Mulled Wine

SERVES 4–6

10 whole cloves
10 allspice berries
1 lemon, or to taste
2 oranges, unwaxed
3 whole star anise
2 cinnamon sticks, plus extra sticks to decorate
¼ teaspoon ground mace
750ml fruity red wine
60g caster sugar, or to taste

Lightly crush the whole cloves and the allspice berries using a pestle and mortar.

Cut the zest off the lemon in a spiral strip. Juice the lemon and one of the oranges. Cut the other orange into slices, keeping the skin on.

Put all the ingredients into a large saucepan, reserving some of the orange slices for decorating the glasses, and slowly bring to a simmer. Stir occasionally to make sure the sugar has dissolved. Reduce the heat to as low as possible and leave to steep for 10 minutes or longer. Taste and adjust the sugar/lemon content, depending on how sweet you want the wine.

Serve the hot wine in heatproof glasses each decorated with a cinnamon stick and a slice of orange.

If you come home from a long walk in the snow and would like something to warm you up quickly, try this recipe. I remember being served a cup of tea with rum after getting caught in a snowstorm, and in that moment, I thought there couldn't be anything better! (For a photograph, see page 164.)

Tee mit Rum
Tea with Rum

Brew 1 mug of tea and let it steep for about 5 minutes.

If serving the tea in a glass, you can make it appear more enticing by moistening the rim with water and dipping it in granulated sugar.

When the tea is ready, pour it into the prepared glass, if using, then add the rum and muscovado sugar. Serve with the slice of lemon and enjoy!

SERVES 1

English Breakfast or Assam tea
granulated sugar (optional)
1 tablespoon spiced rum
2 teaspoons muscovado sugar
1 lemon slice, to serve

Containing coffee, chocolate, cherries and cream, this luxurious drink could justifiably be described as a liquid Black Forest gateau! When pouring your coffee, remember to leave enough space in the mug to add the other ingredients.

Kaffee Kirsch
Black Forest Coffee

SERVES 1

1 mug freshly brewed coffee
1 tablespoon Kirsch
1 teaspoon sugar
milk, to taste (optional)
1 dollop whipped cream
chocolate flakes, to serve

To your mug of coffee, add the Kirsch, sugar and milk to taste (if using). Top with the whipped cream and sprinkle with chocolate flakes.

Marzipan und Nusspasten
Marzipan and Nut Pastes 192

Kuvertüre
Dipping Chocolate 193

Vanille-Zucker
Vanilla Sugar 194

Zimt-Zucker
Cinnamon Sugar 194

Lebkuchen-Gewürz
Gingerbread Spice 195

Rumtopf
Traditional Rum Pot 198

Meerrettich-Sahne
Horseradish Cream 199

Salzteig
Salt Dough 201

From the German Pantry

Marzipan is perhaps the best-known nut paste in Germany, where it is widely used in baking, but also for modelling into fruit and vegetable shapes, such as Marzipan Potatoes (see page 48), chocolate-covered loaves and other traditional treats. The more almonds the paste contains, the higher the quality. The highest grade is made with two parts almonds to one part sugar, which is the recipe I give here. However, the type used for baking in Germany often has equal amounts of sugar and almonds. Marzipan in the UK usually contains three parts sugar to one part almonds, so it is worth making your own. The result will be less sweet and hold its shape better.

Marzipan und Nusspasten
Marzipan and Nut Pastes

MAKES 450G

For almond paste (marzipan)
300g almonds
150g icing sugar, plus extra if needed
1 teaspoon rose water (optional)

For pistachio paste
300g pistachios
150g icing sugar, plus extra if needed
1 teaspoon orange blossom water (optional)

For hazelnut paste
150g hazelnuts
150g almonds
150g icing sugar, plus extra if needed

Using a nut grinder, blender or food processor, grind your chosen nuts. If using a blender or processor, take care not to let the nuts get too warm, or the oil will separate and you'll end up with nut butter.

Add the icing sugar and flavouring (if desired), then blend or process for several minutes, until a lumpy paste forms. You might need to switch off the machine and free the paste from the blades several times during the process. Also, depending on the size of your machine, you might need to work in batches.

Turn the lumpy paste onto a work surface and knead by hand until it forms a smooth ball. You might need to add a bit of water if the paste is too crumbly and dry. If the paste is too wet, add a bit of icing sugar.

Place the finished nut paste in an airtight container and set aside to rest in a cool place for a few hours before using. All these nut pastes will keep for several weeks in the fridge.

The addition of fat to melted chocolate makes it a little more fluid and forgiving when used for dipping or coating baked goods. When I was little, my mother used to buy ready-made dipping chocolate that came in a little metal bucket, complete with a handle.

Kuvertüre
Dipping Chocolate

Break the chocolate into small pieces and place it in a heatproof bowl, together with the coconut oil. Melt the chocolate in 10-second bursts on High in a microwave, stirring it between each burst. Alternatively, you can use a bain-marie: sit the bowl over a pan of simmering water – it must not actually touch the water – and stir as it melts. With both methods, the chocolate should not get warmer than 34ºC, or you might have to temper it to get good results. (Tempering chocolate involves heating and cooling it in order to change its structure and appearance, making it smoother and glossier.)

The melted chocolate can be used straight away. Alternatively, you can spread it out on a sheet of baking paper to set. It will keep for several weeks stored in a cool place. For reheating, break the coating chocolate into little pieces and melt once more, as above.

MAKES 300G

300g dark chocolate (at least 50 per cent cocoa solids)
1 teaspoon coconut oil or cocoa butter

Vanilla sugar, often sold in sachets, is one of those ingredients that you'll find in every German household. However, making your own is quite simple. The method below uses a split pod and seeds, but you can also use empty pods (having used the seeds for another purpose), or you can leave a whole, unopened pod in a jar of sugar for a couple of weeks. Do not leave the latter in the jar too long or it will become dry and brittle and you then won't be able to use it other dishes. Cinnamon sugar is very tasty sprinkled on waffles, pancakes and the like, or to flavour fillings for apple pie or crumble. It can also be nice sprinkled on a dollop of whipped cream.

Vanille-Zucker
Vanilla Sugar

MAKES 1 JAR

1 vanilla pod, split open lengthways and seeds scraped out
caster sugar, as needed

Place the vanilla pod and its seeds in a tall screwtop jar. Cover with caster sugar, seal tightly, shake well and store in a cupboard or larder until needed. Let the vanilla infuse for at least a week or 2 before using. The vanilla pod can stay in the jar until the sugar is used up.

Zimt-Zucker
Cinnamon Sugar

MAKES 1 JAR

1 tablespoon ground cinnamon
200g caster sugar

Place the cinnamon in a screwtop jar and top up with sugar until the jar is almost full. Seal tightly and shake well. Store until needed.

There are many recipes for gingerbread spice, but I particularly like the combination of flavours below, especially the light heat that comes from the pepper and allspice. Ginger was not very common when I was baking with my mother and brother in Germany, so it does not feature in this mixture.

Lebkuchen-Gewürz
Gingerbread Spice

Place all the spices in a small screwtop jar. Seal tightly and shake well to combine. Use as needed.

MAKES 1 JAR

5 tablespoons ground cinnamon
2 teaspoons ground cloves
1 teaspoon ground aniseed
½ teaspoon ground nutmeg
½ teaspoon ground cardamom
1 teaspoon ground coriander
½ teaspoon ground allspice
½ teaspoon ground black pepper

Christmas on German TV

Back in the 1970s, my father worked long hours. He was a master locksmith and welder in a metal construction company, and the work was physically demanding. In the evenings, watching TV therefore featured quite strongly in our family life, although we also played a lot of card games and board games. At that time there were just three TV channels in Germany, all of them state-operated, showing an eclectic mix of news, game shows, culture programmes, murder mysteries and Hollywood movies (which were dubbed into German). Advertising was strictly regulated and sparse – commercials were only shown between the programmes, with no ad breaks disrupting movies or TV shows.

In the run-up to Christmas and New Year's Eve, there was more music on TV than usual, and there were more movies. As a family, we always looked forward to this festive change in programming: my parents liked the classic Hollywood musicals and I suppose I got my earliest doses of jazz from watching television at this time of year, too. But I most looked forward to seeing the adventure movies that were broadcast at this time of year. The ones based on the books of Jules Verne were always among them – *Around the World in 80 Days* and *20,000 Leagues Under the Sea* – as were pirate classics like *Treasure Island* or anything starring Errol Flynn, such as *Robin Hood*. As neither video recorders nor streaming services existed yet, we looked forward to watching these epic movies on TV year on year.

My father, my mother and me at Christmas..

Me having fun climbing the snow piles that accumulated when we cleared our back yard.

Alcohol and sugar are very good for preserving fruit, and using both over the course of the year is a great way to build a store of seasonal fruit that can be used in many desserts when fresh alternatives are harder to come by. I like to start my layered jar of fruit in the spring, when fresh strawberries appear, then add peaches, cherries, blackberries and other soft fruits, apricots, plums – you name it! – as they become available. Rumtopf needs to mature for at least two months, so don't leave your preserving later than October or it won't be ready in time for Christmas. You'll need a large jar (at least 1 litre) with a lid for this – fermentation jars are perfect.

Rumtopf
Traditional Rum Pot

MAKES 1 POT

fruit in season (basically, anything that holds together well – not bananas)
caster sugar or granulated sugar, as needed
rum, as needed

Clean, pit and de-stem your fruit as necessary. Anything bigger than a walnut should be cut in half or quartered.

Place a layer of fruit in a large screwtop jar, add a few tablespoons of sugar and enough rum to cover both by at least 1cm (you want your Rumtopf to infuse, not ferment). Seal tightly and store in a cool, dark place.

Add extra layers of fruit, sugar and rum as new fruit becomes available.

If pure horseradish is too strong for you, this recipe should do the trick. The cream mellows the heat of the horseradish while enhancing its finer flavours. It is excellent with smoked fish, meats and sausages.

Meerrettich-Sahne
Horseradish Cream

Place the cream in a bowl and stir in the horseradish. Season to taste with lemon juice and salt. The result should hold its shape, so don't make it too liquid.

Transfer to a small screwtop jar, seal tightly, then label and date. If stored in the fridge, this will keep for well over a week.

MAKES 1 SMALL JAR

150ml double cream
60g horseradish, freshly and finely grated, or from a jar
lemon juice, as needed
salt

TIP:

For an elegant condiment to serve with hot smoked trout, use this recipe, but whip the cream before adding the horseradish to it. (For a photograph, see page 136.)

This dough is not edible, but it's perfect for making Christmas decorations and ornaments. It can be coloured with food colouring and shaped by using biscuit cutters, stencils or *Springerle* moulds, or even free-hand sculpting – you can make br wreaths, for example. or press dried leaves into the surface of the dough to create an imprint. Once shaped, the dough can be decorated with water-based paints in whatever patterns or designs you fancy. Once they are dry, seal your salt dough ornaments with a coat of varnish.

Salzteig
Salt Dough

Line a baking sheet with baking paper.

Place the flour, salt, water and oil in a bowl and mix together. Transfer to a floured work surface and knead until smooth. If you want to colour some portions of your dough, add a few drops of food colouring to a small ball of dough and knead in well.

Roll the dough out until 5mm thick, then cut out your decorations. If you want to hang them from your Christmas tree, pierce 2 holes with a skewer so that a string or ribbon can be threaded through later.

Set the shapes aside on the prepared sheet and leave in a warm place to air-dry for several days. Alternatively, place in an oven preheated to its lowest temperature, propping the door open with a wooden spoon as it shouldn't exceed 70°C. Leave for 1 hour, then close the door, increase the oven temperature to 120°C fan/gas mark 1 and bake for 2 hours. Set aside to cool.

Once the shapes are cold and dry, paint them as you wish, or simply give them a coat of varnish. String or ribbon can be added if you want to hang them up.

MAKES ABOUT 570G

220g plain flour, plus extra for dusting
200g salt
150ml water
1 tablespoon vegetable oil
food colouring (optional)

Index

A
advent 7–8, 72, 108–9
almonds
  Christmas Linzer Torte 93
  cinnamon stars 25
  honey gingerbread 54
  Jürgen's orange Yule log 85–7
  Linzer Christmas biscuits 29
  little Bethmanns 20
  marzipan and nut pastes 192
  Miller-style trout 135
  roast almonds 173
  special gingerbread 51
  vanilla crescents 40
  yogurt stollen 103
aniseed
  aniseed biscuits 33
  Springerle 58–9
apples
  baked apples 165
  Christmas apple pie 89
  cinnamon fruit cake in a jar 97
  fruit salad 166
  Sauerkraut with apples and wine 157
apricot jam
  tree cake 80–1

B
bacon
  potato salad 159
  Sauerkraut with apples and wine 157
baking ammonia 59
baking powder 59
baking wafers 15
bananas
  fruit salad 166
Baumkuchen-Torte 80–1
beef
  Christmas beef roulades 144–5
Belgian waffles 179
Bethmännchen 20
bicarbonate of soda 59
biscuits
  aniseed biscuits 33
  black and white biscuits 30–2
  butter biscuits 19
  cheese biscuits 57
  chocolate pretzels 47
  cinnamon stars 25
  coconut macaroons 16
  filled gingerbread hearts 53
  hazelnut macaroons 15
  Hilda-Brötle 44
  honey gingerbread 54
  Lebkuchen 50–4
  Linzer Christmas biscuits 29
  little Bethmanns 20
  marzipan potatoes 48
  piped biscuits 34–5
  pistachio and orange biscuits 43
  raising agents for 59
  rum balls 39
  special gingerbread 51
  Springerle 58–9
  swaddled biscuits 22
  vanilla crescents 40
  walnut and coffee biscuits 26
black and white biscuits 30–2
Black Forest coffee 188
Brade, William 72
bread
  Christmas scones 107
  crusty Black Forest loaf 113
  dough men 108–9
  gammon in a bread crust 153–4
  rye bread 118
  sourdough starters 114–16
  sweet filled buns 104
  yogurt stollen 103
Buchteln 104
buns
  sweet filled buns 104
butter biscuits 19

C
cabbage
  fermented cabbage 155
  Sauerkraut 155
  Sauerkraut with apples and wine 157
cakes 77
  cinnamon fruit cake in a jar 97
  honey cake or lekach 94
  Jürgen's orange Yule log 85–7
  mulled wine cake 78
  tree cake 80–1
canapés
  smoked fish canapés 134
caraway seeds
  cheese biscuits 57
Cheddar
  cheese biscuits 57
cheese
  cheese biscuits 57
  Spätzle with cheese and onions 162
cherries, glacé
  honey gingerbread 54
chestnuts
  Christmas beef roulades 144–5
chicken in white wine 127
chocolate
  chocolate pretzels 47
  chocolate waffles with Kirsch cream 130–1
  Christmas Pavlova 138–9

coconut macaroons 16
dipping chocolate 193
filled gingerbread hearts 53
gingerbread bites 182
Jürgen's orange Yule log 85–7
piped biscuits 34–5
rum balls 39
tree cake 80–1
walnut and coffee biscuits 26
Christmas beef roulades 144–5
Christmas Eve 123, 150–1
Christmas markets 171, 180
Christmas Pavlova 138–9
Christmas scones 107
Christmas television 196
cinnamon
　cinnamon fruit cake in a jar 97
　cinnamon stars 25
　cinnamon sugar 194
　roast almonds 173
cocoa
　black and white biscuits 30–2
　Christmas Linzer Torte 93
　Linzer Christmas biscuits 29
coconut macaroons 16
coffee
　Black Forest coffee 188
　walnut and coffee biscuits 26
cranberries
　Christmas beef roulades 144–5
cream
　Belgian waffles 179
　Black Forest coffee 188
　chocolate waffles with Kirsch cream 130–1
　Christmas Pavlova 138–9
　horseradish cream 199

D
decorations
　salt dough 201
dough men 108–9
drinks
　Black Forest coffee 188
　mulled wine 186
　tea with rum 187

E
egg whites
　Christmas Pavlova 138–9
　coconut macaroons 16
　hazelnut macaroons 15
eggs
　egg noodles from South-West Germany 161

F
filled gingerbread hearts 53
fish
　Miller-style trout 135
　smoked fish canapés 134
fruit
　cinnamon fruit cake in a jar 97
　fruit salad 166
　traditional rum pot 198
　wine jelly with fruit 149
fruit, dried
　baked apples 165
　Christmas scones 107
　dough men 108–9
　sweet filled buns 104
　yogurt stollen 103

G
gammon in a bread crust 153–4
gingerbread
　filled gingerbread hearts 53
　gingerbread bites 182
　gingerbread hearts 175–6
　gingerbread house 62–71
　gingerbread spice 195
　honey gingerbread 54
　special gingerbread 51
Glühwein 78, 186
　mulled wine cake 78
Gruyère
　Spätzle with cheese and onions 162

H
hazelnuts
　hazelnut macaroons 15
　marzipan and nut pastes 192
　special gingerbread 51
Hilda-Brötle 44
honey
　filled gingerbread hearts 53
　gingerbread house 62–71
　honey cake or lekach 94
　honey gingerbread 54
horseradish cream 199
　smoked fish canapés 134

J
jelly
　wine jelly with fruit 149
juniper berries
　fermented cabbage 155

K
Kappel 90
Kirsch
　Black Forest coffee 188
　chocolate waffles with Kirsch cream 130–1
　fruit salad 166
Knecht Ruprecht 21

L
lamb's lettuce salad 143
Lebkuchen 50–4

INDEX

filled gingerbread hearts 53
gingerbread hearts 175–6
gingerbread spice 195
honey gingerbread 54
special gingerbread 51
lettuce
   lamb's lettuce salad 143
Linzer Christmas biscuits 29
Linzer Torte
   Christmas Linzer Torte 93
little Bethmanns 20

M
macaroons
   coconut 16
   hazelnut 15
Magenbrot 182
marzipan
   little Bethmanns 20
   marzipan and nut pastes 192
   marzipan figurines 63, 69
   marzipan potatoes 48
   swaddled biscuits 22
Meerrettich-Sahne 199
meringue
   Christmas Pavlova 138–9
Miller-style trout 135
mulled wine 186
   mulled wine cake 78
mushrooms
   chicken in white wine 127
music 72, 90–1

N
noodles 160
   egg noodles from South-West Germany 161
   Spätzle with cheese and onions 162

O
onions
   potato cakes 185
   potato salad 159
   Spätzle with cheese and onions 162
oranges
   Christmas Pavlova 138–9
   fruit salad 166
   Jürgen's orange Yule log 85–7
   pistachio and orange biscuits 43

P
parsnips
   mashed potato 158
pears
   fruit salad 166
peel, mixed
   Christmas apple pie 89
   Christmas scones 107
   honey gingerbread 54
   mulled wine cake 78
   pistachio and orange biscuits 43
   special gingerbread 51
   yogurt stollen 103
peppers
   potato salad 159
piped biscuits 34–5
pistachios
   marzipan and nut pastes 192
   pistachio and orange biscuits 43
potatoes
   mashed potato 158
   Miller-style trout 135
   potato cakes 185
   potato croquettes 163
   potato salad 159
pretzels
   chocolate pretzels 47
prunes
   Christmas Pavlova 138–9

R
raising agents 59
Reibekuchen 185
Roggenbrot 118
roulades
   Christmas beef roulades 144–5
royal icing
   gingerbread hearts 175–6
   gingerbread house 62–71
rum
   filled gingerbread hearts 53
   rum balls 39
   tea with rum 187
   traditional rum pot 198
   yogurt stollen 103
rye bread 118

S
salads
   lamb's lettuce salad 143
   potato salad 159
salmon
   smoked fish canapés 134
salt dough 201
Sauerkraut 155
   Sauerkraut with apples and wine 157
Schütz, Heinrich 72
scones
   Christmas scones 107
semolina dumpling soup 126
smoked fish canapés 134
soup
   semolina dumpling soup 126
sourdough starters 114–16
Spätzle 161
   Spätzle with cheese and onions 162
spices
   Christmas apple pie 89
   Christmas Linzer Torte 93
   gingerbread spice 195

honey cake or lekach 94
mulled wine 186
mulled wine cake 78
yogurt stollen 103
Springerle 58–9
squash
   Christmas beef roulades 144–5
St Martin's Day 108–9, 119
St Nicholas Day 21
sugar
   cinnamon sugar 194
   roast almonds 173
   vanilla sugar 194
swaddled biscuits 22

T
tarts & pies 77
   Christmas apple pie 89
   Christmas Linzer Torte 93
tea with rum 187
trout
   Miller-style trout 135

V
vanilla sugar 194
   Hilda-Brötle 44
   vanilla crescents 40
vegetables
   chicken in white wine 127
   Christmas beef roulades 144–5
vinaigrette
   potato salad 159
Vorfreude 119

W
waffles
   Belgian waffles 179
   chocolate waffles with Kirsch cream 130–1
walnuts
   baked apples 165
   Christmas Pavlova 138–9
   lamb's lettuce salad 143
   walnut and coffee biscuits 26
Weckmänner 108–9
wine
   chicken in white wine 127
   Christmas beef roulades 144–5
   mulled wine 186
   Sauerkraut with apples and wine 157
   wine jelly with fruit 149

Y
yogurt stollen 103

Danke
Thank You

First of all, I want to thank you, my readers, because it is your warm reception of my first book that gave me the opportunity to tell the stories and write the recipes you are now holding in your hands.

I was overjoyed to be asked to write a book about the food and experiences of my childhood, specifically focussing on the time around Christmas. Thank you, Joanna Copestick, for making this book happen and for providing the best team I could have wished for. Alex Stetter, it was a pleasure to have you as my editor, understanding the German intricacies and always finding a way of presenting them to an English-speaking audience.

Classic German cookbooks don't contain many illustrations, but this book is different, as it is not just a cookbook – it aims to re-create some of the atmosphere of those weeks in December in my childhood home. Every time I look at the photos, I am amazed how well they capture my German Christmas, and for this I thank the team I am so honoured to have worked with. Katie Marshall and Maria Gurevich, thank you for cooking and baking my recipes with such dedication and precision. Tony Hutchinson, I could just spend all the time allocated to photo shoots just looking at your props – and all the items come with ideas for how to use them to enhance the baked goods on display, with so much sensitivity to the cultural context. My writing and the magical imagery have to be brought together on paper – thank you, Jaz Bahra, for doing that so beautifully. And thank you to production manager Caroline Alberti for turning these pages into an actual book.

All this baking, cooking and arranging of food needs to be photographed, and I couldn't have wished for a better person to do that than Maja Smend. Thank you for your creativity and passion. In your photography you not only captured the essence of this book, but also the immense joy of everyone working on it.

Thank you, Katherine Stonehouse, my agent. You are always there with your vision and belief in me, ready to help and organise.

Thank you to Prospectus and their CEO Peter Beeby for all your support over the years. You have given me time off to be able to develop and test the recipes in this book and were always happy for me to try them out on you!

A special thank you to Paul Williams, my local butcher (Bramptons, in Brighton) and your colleagues Fran and Steve, for all your support in developing some of the meaty recipes, for the chats about food, and for promoting me to your customers.

Thanks also to Rachel Barnard and her family, who are always keen to taste my recipes, for their support and thoughtful feedback.

This book is all about my childhood Christmas experiences and time spent with my close family. I want to thank my mother Erna and my father Harro for giving me the space to grow up together with my brother Günter. Your openness to experiments – and the abundance of materials at home – was an amazing start for my baking journey, but it manifested itself in so many areas. Now I understand well what patience and love it takes to be kind when you return home from work to find your tools in disarray, or that new packet of nails completely depleted.

Dear Benjamin, thank you for your appreciation and your thorough and in-depth criticism during recipe development. Your fine palate and keen eye helped me a lot.

Finally, I want to thank you, my dearest wife Sophia, who supported me all along with your love and shared your visions and ideas for this book. We had many discussions about the shape, colour and flavour of individual recipes, and you inspired me and moved me to make the gingerbread house what it is.

Sophia and Benjamin, you were the best coaching team in the world, this book wouldn't be the same without your love and contributions.